INSTRUMENTAL

jazz ears

aural skills for the improvising musician

by thom mason

ISBN-13: 978-0-7935-7940-2
ISBN-10: 0-7935-7940-6

7777 W. BLUEMOUND RD. P.O. BOX 13819 MILWAUKEE, WI 53213

In Australia Contact:
Hal Leonard Australia Pty. Ltd.
4 Lentara Court
Cheltenham, Victoria, 3192 Australia
Email: ausadmin@halleonard.com

Visit Hal Leonard Online at
www.halleonard.com

Contents

Introduction

This is a book about hearing music without having to use a piano, guitar, or any other instrument to help you. One of the goals is to look at a piece of music and hear it in your head. Another is to be able to listen to a piece of music and recognize what's going on without having any written music in front of you. We are not suggesting that you will be able to look at a page of music and hear everything you see instantly, nor will you necessarily be able to listen to a performance and immediately recognize everything. Throughout all of recorded history only a very few individuals have ever been able to do that. What we *are* saying is that if you study and apply the materials in this book, you have a good chance of becoming much better at these things than you are now.

All good jazz musicians have had to learn to do this at some point in their careers, many by trial and error. There's nothing wrong with trial and error—it's actually a very good teacher. It just takes a lot of time and it isn't always the most efficient way to learn something, especially how to be a good jazz musician. What we're going to do in this book is share a lifetime of playing and teaching experiences that can help you in your quest to achieve your musical goals. Some of the things in this book will likely seem a bit unusual at first, but if you give them a chance and master them, they will pay off. All you need is a sense of dedication and a willingness to put in the practice time.

How to Use This Book

The material found in this book is intended to be studied in order, but you also have the option to look through the entire book first, and, if you find a topic you're really interested in, practice it and begin using it right away. If you choose this second approach, as you get better, you'll hopefully come back to the book, find something else that interests you, and work on new topics. The choice is yours.

One thing is certain: you need to be able to read basic musical notation (including rhythms utilizing sixteenth notes), but you don't need to be a great sight reader. Most of this material is intended to be practiced, then applied. And while it helps to have some skills on either the piano or guitar, that also isn't a requirement. It has been observed that many students who didn't play piano or guitar at all have done very well applying these materials to their practice.

Mastering the material will take time. It can't be assimilated all at once. The ideal practice session should last fifteen to thirty minutes each day. Any longer and you run the risk of getting burned out. And besides, you can't cram ear-training skills anyway—you have to give them time to become second nature.

Some musicians find it useful to practice ear training in the middle of their daily instrumental warm-up routines. It gives their chops a chance to rest for a few minutes, but keeps them focused on performing and mastering the music. However you wish to do it, take it in small pieces and you *will* get there.

How the Book Is Organized

There are two main sections to this book. The first section explores basic problems associated with reading jazz notation, interval studies, reading and practicing melodies, singing root movements, outlining chords, and learning chord scales, as they relate to the major scale. All of this is done by focusing on music in major keys. The second section of the book expands the materials on reading jazz notation to include performing articulations characteristic of jazz (i.e., fall, glissando, ghosted note, etc.), before moving on to more studies of the topics covered in the first section, but as they relate to music in minor keys. In addition, the last chapter contains material on how to create guide-tone lines: skeletal melodies that act as road maps through the chord progressions of jazz tunes. This is followed by a syllabus called the "Chord Chart Syllabus," which contains examples from some of the more important and famous chord progressions found in tunes you are likely to encounter as you develop your musical skills.

About the CD

There are two kinds of tracks on the CD. Most tracks demonstrate the different techniques explained in the book so you can hear how to apply them. These tracks are recorded so you can listen to the voice track, sing along with the voice for practice, and then eliminate the voice entirely so you can practice on your own with the pre-recorded accompaniment on each track. Remove the voice part by turning down the volume on the right channel. Also note that many of the tracks are sung with rhythm only, though the exercise in the book will often consist of a melody. This is done so that you may concentrate on rhythm and articulation first. Once you have this aspect learned, you may then challenge yourself by singing the actual notated pitches. The second kind of track contains dictation exercises. These consist of intervals or chord-scales that you are asked to identify. Both kinds of track help to reinforce your ability to hear and recognize melodic and scale material without having to see the notes on paper.

When CD tracks are called for in the book you will see the following symbol:

This icon will be followed by a brief explanation of what the track covers and how to practice it. Most of the tracks are recorded at moderate tempos for ease of practice. There's another practical reason for this: at faster tempos the chord roots and solfege names can become too difficult to pronounce. Besides, once you've practiced something and really understand it, the tempo won't matter as far as your hearing and understanding is concerned.

You might be interested in knowing that when it came time to make a decision about who we would get to record the voice tracks, we chose to get someone less gifted as a vocalist, but perhaps a little more believable because the performances wouldn't be flawless. So we picked the author to record the tracks because, quite honestly, "If I can't do what I'm asking you to do, then why am I asking you to do it?"

I sincerely hope you will find this book helpful and wish you every success in developing your *Jazz Ears*.

Thom David Mason

About the Author

Dr. Thom Mason has been teaching since 1977 at the University of Southern California, where he founded the Department of Jazz Studies, and was its chairman from 1983 to 1996. He is a tenured senior professor of music, teaching undergraduate ear training and jazz history, and directs the doctoral program for Jazz Studies. In addition, he is an artist/clinician and educational and instrument design consultant for the Jupiter Band Instrument Company of Austin, Texas. As a performer, Dr. Mason has appeared throughout the United States, and in Canada, Germany, Israel, Japan, Taiwan, New Zealand, and Australia. He has also recorded four jazz albums under his own name and appeared on several other jazz albums as a guest performer.

Section One

1 Hearing Jazz Rhythms and Articulations, Part One

Musicians make mistakes reading music for two main reasons: 1) they don't recognize the way the music looks, which means they see symbols on the page, but don't know what the symbols actually mean (in some cases these are rhythmic symbols, in others they are articulation symbols); and 2) they haven't really mastered their instruments yet (so they make technical mistakes). Professional studio musicians rarely make mistakes for the second reason, which leaves us with the first: recognizing the way the music looks. Any time studio professionals are given a new piece of music to read, the first thing they do is skim through it to look for unfamiliar or unusual rhythms and articulations. Next, they may sing the music softly to themselves before the recording session begins. They're drawing on their years of experience to see them through; but you may not have that experience, at least not yet. That's the reason why the following system for reading and articulating rhythmic symbols was developed. When using this system you should be able to reduce dramatically the possibility of making rhythmic and articulation mistakes the first time you play through a piece. This means that, to paraphrase the great jazz saxophonist Charlie Parker, you'll be concentrating on playing the music instead of playing the notes.

You might be surprised to know that when jazz began to find its way into the public schools many years ago, jazz educators discovered that there wasn't any standardized notation for big band arrangements. Downbeat jazz quarter notes might be marked with a marcato symbol (∧) on one occasion, and with an accent mark (>) on another. Sometimes this happened within the same arrangement! As another example, if you wanted to know how long a quarter note was, some arrangements used dashes while others used words like "long," "legato," or "full." It got to a point where some arrangements came to look something like a road map, and somewhere along the way the music itself got lost (pun intended). Band directors became bogged down in arguments over just how long an accented eighth note should be compared to an unaccented, staccato quarter note (this is a sad commentary, but true). Today we seem to have come full-circle in our quest to perform music written in European classical notation that is intended to be performed quite differently from how it looks.

Most of the important developments in jazz rhythmic interpretation over the past one hundred years stem from an aural tradition in which musicians play something by listening to how it sounds rather than looking at it. Thus, it only seems logical to return to that aural tradition and ask ourselves, "What does it sound like?" first, and then look at the music.

The Legato Attack

One of the primary ways jazz differs from classical music is in how notes begin, or how they are attacked. Classically trained musicians prefer to start notes with a moderately hard attack that sounds something like "tah." Jazz musicians prefer a softer and lighter legato attack that sounds something like "doo." In fact, brass players often refer to this as using the "du-tongue" to distinguish it from the traditional way of starting a note. This doesn't mean the traditional attack isn't used, it just means that it's generally reserved for heavier, more percussive accents.

At this point, some of the sounds associated with scat singing can be very helpful in understanding the differences between these two attacks. Scat words like **Doo, dah,** and **duh** all convey a sense of the soft attack favored in jazz, while **Too** and **Tah** suggest the traditional attack. Compare **Doo dah, Doo dah** or **Doo duh, Doo duh** with **Too Too, Too Too** or **Tah Tah, Tah Tah**. You immediately notice the softer quality of the **doo** patterns and the percussive quality of the traditional attacks. And it should come as no surprise that great jazz vocalists from Louis Armstrong to Ella Fitzgerald, Sarah Vaughan, Bobby McFerrin, and Kurt Elling consistently use the more relaxed sounds in their scat solos, which is significant for another reason: scat singing is a purely "jazz" way of performing—it has no European counterpart.

How the Music Feels

Because most musicians today come to jazz with a background in pop and rock music, they are familiar with music performed with a straight feel and somewhat less familiar with music performed with a swing feel. In the straight feel, the beat is assumed to be divided into two equal halves. With swing feel, the beat is divided into two unequal parts. The first eighth is equal to about two thirds of the beat, with the second eighth equal to about one third of the beat. We will begin by discussing jazz articulations in relation to the straight feel, then move to those same jazz articulations performed with a swing feel.

Full and Stopped Releases

Just as there are two basic ways to start a note, there are two basic ways to release a note, the **full release** and the **stopped release**. When using the full release, a note is allowed to die away naturally. The stopped release is used frequently by jazz musicians and creates an abrupt or clipped ending to the note. In reading jazz notation we use doo and dah to define full-value quarter notes.

Doo (— or ≥) = downbeat with full release   **dah** (— or ≥) = upbeat with full release

It doesn't matter if the note is accented or not. There is a shorthand symbol for downbeats, which is capital "D"; for upbeats the shorthand symbol is a lower case "d" to show that the note is on the back half of the beat.

The following example illustrates downbeat and upbeat full-value quarter notes with full release. Although all notes are full-value, you'll notice that some are accented. Pick any pitch you want and sing these articulations to yourself. As you sing them, stress the accented notes in measures 1 and 3 to show the change in dynamics.

The Jazz Quarter Note

The **jazz quarter note** is different from the full-value quarter note. This is a staccato note that occurs with considerable frequency in jazz, particularly in swing and blues tunes where it often appears side-by-side with full-value quarter notes. The jazz quarter note has a value equal to about two-thirds of a normal quarter note. And because it's a stopped note, it ends with "t." "Doo" becomes "Doot" and "dah" becomes "daht." The important thing to remember is to make the note short, but not too short or it will sound like a staccato eighth note.

Doot (· or ∸) = a shortened downbeat jazz quarter note

daht (· or ∸) = a shortened upbeat jazz quarter note

Upbeat Jazz Quarter Notes

The next example shows some **upbeat jazz quarter notes** followed by rests. When these notes are followed by a rest they should automatically be given an accent, unless specifically marked as legato. This is standard practice, even if there is no accent mark used.

Note the two different ways they have been notated. The first two bars show one notation, and the third bar shows another. In all cases they should be accented and stopped to be performed correctly.

The Marcato Quarter Note

The **marcato** sign (∧) is another form of accent commonly found in jazz. It indicates that the length of the note is the same as the jazz quarter note, but more heavily accented. From moderately slow to fast tempos, marcato symbols are used to indicate to the player to stress a note.

Dat (∧) = A marcato, accented short quarter note.

"**Dat**" rhymes with "cat" or "bat." There is no need to use different names for downbeats or upbeats because this symbol only has to do with accent, not duration. The following example shows an on-the-beat marcato on beat 4 of the first bar. It's also louder than the first three notes.

Here's an example showing an off-the-beat marcato note in the first bar. It should be louder than the first two notes and also louder than the two notes that follow it.

The following one-note exercises review the articulations presented so far. On the CD, before the exercises begin, a reference pitch is sung. You should do the same thing whenever you practice or plan to sing through something rhythmic. Listen to the track, then sing along with the voice. (Remember that you can also eliminate the voice track by turning down the right channel.) The rhythms and accents you sing are reinforced by the drum part. This helps confirm that what you're singing is correct. Finally, as you practice, make sure you remember to give accented notes a slightly stronger push, just as you would if you were playing your instrument or scat singing a melodic line. And don't forget to give the marcato accent an even stronger push.

TRACK 1
Exercises 1–4

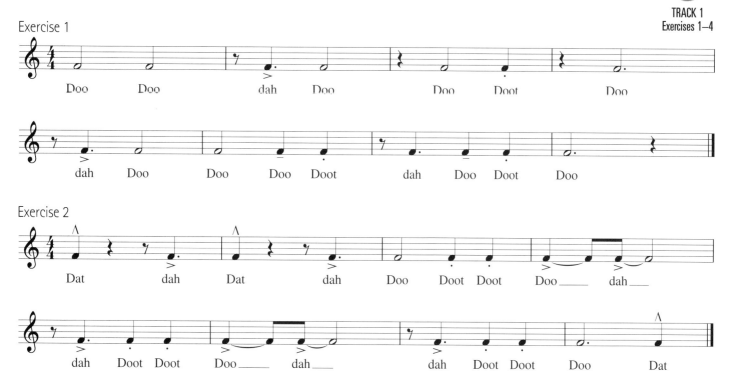

Exercise 3

Doo   Doot Doot   Doo___   dah___   Doo   Doot Doo Doot   Doo   dah

Doot Doo   dah___   Doot Doot   Doo   Doo___   dah___   Dat

Exercise 4

Doo   dah___   Dat   Doo   dah___   Dat   daht daht daht dah___   Doo

daht   Doo   daht   Doo   Doo   dah___   Doo

When you get a new arrangement to play in your band or combo, look for these articulations in the music and sing them to yourself. Remember that you don't have to sing the actual pitches, just chant the rhythms. Once you see and recognize them, you'll play them correctly on your instrument.

Legato and Staccato Eighth Notes

Eighth notes use the same syllables we used for quarter notes, so when we see a string of eighth notes intended to be performed **legato**, we sing them as "Doo-dah, Doo-dah, Doo-dah, Doo," as in the following example.

Doo dah Doo dah Doo dah Doo dah   Doo   daht___   Doo   Doo dah Doo   Doo dah___

When we want to perform them **staccato**, we use the syllable "Dit." In fact, we use "Dit" for staccato sixteenth notes as well, even though they should actually be even shorter. Most jazz musicians don't make any distinction between staccato eighths and sixteenths. Our next example shows the same four measures of music using staccato eighth notes instead of legato eighth notes.

Dit dit Dit dit Dit dit Dit dah   Doo   daht___   Doo   Dit dit Doo   Dit dah___

Staccato eighths are fairly common in Latin jazz, jazz-rock, and fusion. They aren't very common in swing music.

Latin Jazz

The melodies of Latin jazz can sometimes be confusing to interpret because there are two distinct styles for accompanying them: a Brazilian style sometimes called the bossa nova (slow) and samba (medium fast to fast), and a Caribbean or Cuban style sometimes referred to as mambo (slow) and son or salsa (medium fast to fast). Musicians playing Latin jazz in a Brazilian style tend to perform the notes longer than musicians playing music in the Cuban style.

The following melody can have two very different interpretations, one Brazilian and the other Cuban. In this case the articulations make it clear as to what style is called for, but that's not usually the case when looking at lead sheets or tunes in a fake book. The CD track for Exercise 5 is rhythm-only—the exercise is sung on one pitch (E♭). It is good practice to be able to see a melodic line, yet isolate and perform its rhythm and articulations only. Once you have the rhythm solid, to make it more interesting, sing the melodies using the actual pitches. The piano plays a concert E♭ (the tonic, not the first note of the exercise) for you at the start of the track so you can sing the melodies "as written."

TRACK 2
Rhythm only

Exercise 5

In comparing the two styles, you may notice that the Cuban style has a more percussive feel. Sing along with the track to get a better understanding of how articulations affect the way Latin jazz is performed. As you do, notice how the legato notes are supported by the Brazilian style and how the shorter notes are supported by the Cuban style. The longer notes of the Brazilian style can be thought of as "cool Latin jazz," while the shorter, percussive notes of the Cuban style make the same tune seem "hotter."

If you see a large number of staccato notes scattered throughout the music, you're probably performing music in the Cuban style. If you don't see many, it's probably a tune in Brazilian style. If you're not sure which style is right, ask.

Fusion and Jazz/Rock Music

In performing the jazz styles known as fusion and jazz/rock, musicians encounter the same issues concerning quarter notes and eighth notes. Fusion tunes tend to be "cool," while jazz/rock tunes are usually "hot" because they are based on rock rhythms. The next exercise uses a single melody interpreted in both styles.

TRACK 3
Rhythm only

Exercise 6

Dit dit Doo daht   dah _____ dit Dit dit   Dit dit Doo daht   daht

Doo dah Doo daht   dah _____ dah Doo daht   Doo dah Doo daht   daht

The first uses a jazz/rock approach and the second uses a fusion approach. Sing along with the track, then turn off the voice channel and practice along with the drums only. Again, if you want to make the exercise more challenging, sing the melodies using the actual pitches. The piano plays a concert G for you at the start of the track so you can sing the melodies "as written."

Both versions are actually similar, except for the legato eighth notes found in the fusion style. In general, it's safe to say that jazz/rock makes more use of staccato eighth notes and percussive accents than fusion. When you sing through the previous example you will be able to hear that the differences between the two styles is not as dramatic as between Brazilian and Cuban, but it's definitely present.

To Swing or Not to Swing

When jazz music is intended to swing, the music is written in simple notation, but it's not performed "as written." To perform it correctly, jazz musicians divide each quarter note into three equal eighth notes called triplets and tie the first two notes together. In other words, the music on the first line of the next example should be performed as it appears in the second line.

How it is written

Doo dah Doo dah Doo   Doo   dah Doo dah _____   dah Doo dah Doo

How it is played

Doo duh Doo duh Doo   Doo   duh Doo duh _____   duh Doo duh Doo

Immediately you will notice that the rhythmic name for the upbeat eighth note in the swing version is "duh" instead of "dah." This might seem like an arbitrary decision, but it's not. We said earlier that the swing feel is related to triplets with the first eighth note getting two thirds of the beat and the second eighth getting one third of the beat. The syllables used in this text for triplets are "Doo-ee-uh" because "oo," "ee," and "uh" are distinctly different vowel sounds from each other, which makes them easy to isolate and sing.

Relating Swing-feel to Triplets

Although we prefer "Doo-ee-uh," there are many different ways to label triplets. Some musicians say "Tri-ple-et," which is awkward at best. Some say "One-La-Lee, Two-La-Lee," etc., which is an improvement, while still others recommend "One-and-uh, Two-and-uh," etc. The point here is that there isn't any standard agreed-upon way to count them; we should also remember that most of these systems were developed to count rhythms only, not deal with durations or articulations. "Doo-ee-uh" is a direct outgrowth of trying to deal with the legato approach to articulation and handle durations at the same time. Not only that, "Doo-ee-uh" is fairly easy to sing. Repeat "Doo-ee-uh, Doo-ee-uh, Doo-ee-uh, Doo-ee-uh" several times and you will see that for yourself. So that's why "Doo-ee-uh" and "Doo-duh" are related and work well together, as in the next example. This begins with triplets to establish the swing feel then moves to swing eighth notes for the second measure.

Swing feel

Doo ee uh Doo ee uh Doo Doo ee uh Doo duh Doo duh

You can see that "Doo-ee-uh" works nicely for triplets that are slurred together or have legato attacks, but when strong articulations are needed we add the consonant "D" to the beginning of the second and third syllables. When using this system, articulated triplets are represented by "Doo-Dee-duh." These syllables are particularly useful for quarter-note triplets because, when they do occur, they are usually articulated and accented. Both "Doo" and "Dee" are capitalized to show they are placed before the halfway point in the triplet, as in the following example.

Doo Dee duh Doo Doo Dee duh Doo Dee duh Doo

At this point, if you're not sure just how "swing feel" and "triplets" are supposed to sound, listen to Track 4, then re-read this material.

Pickups and Ending Eighth Notes

When a phrase begins with an eighth-note pickup we use "duh" if we want to give it a swing feel and "dah" if we want to give it a straight feel. The next example shows what we're talking about. The top text is used for swing feel and the bottom for straight feel. Only the downbeats (Doo) line up—all the swing upbeats fall later than the straight feel upbeats. Try chanting through the example twice, once with a swing feel and once with a straight feel.

swing: duh Doo duh Doo dut dut dut dut dut duh Doo dut
straight: dah Doo dah Doo daht daht daht daht daht dah Doo daht

When eighth notes end a phrase and are followed by a rest, no matter how long the rest, they are expected to be shortened and receive more weight than conventional eighth notes. That's why the previous example ended with "dut" for the swing feel and "daht" for the straight feel. Either way, the stopped release gives the note weight and body.

The following exercises apply what we've just covered, performing jazz articulations with a swing feel. Go through the exercises, chanting the rhythms on one pitch. The drum parts have been carefully composed to match each exercise. Listen to the track first, then chant along with the voice part, and finally eliminate the voice track and chant the exercises with drums only.

TRACK 4
Exercises 7–12
Rhythm only

Exercise 7

Doo Dee duh Doo Doo dut dut dut Doo duh __ Doo ee uh Doo ee uh Doo Doo duh Doo duh Doo dut

Exercise 8

Doo ee uh Doo duh __ Doo ee uh Doo duh Doo dut duh Doo Dee duh Doo Dee duh Doo Doo dut

Exercise 9

duh Doo ee uh Doo dut　　duh Doo duh Doo dut　　duh Doo ee uh Doo duh Doo dut　　duh Doo duh Doo dut

Exercise 10

Doo Doot Doo dut　　duh Doo　　Doot Doot　　Doo ee uh Doo duh Doo dut　　dut　　dut　　dut

Exercise 11

Doo　　Doot　　Doo duh Doo dut　　Doo ee uh　Doo dut　　duh Doot Doo duh　Doo duh Doo dut

Exercise 12

Doo dut　　duh Doot Doot　　Doo duh Doo　duh ___　　Doo Dee duh Doo Dee duh　Doo　dut

Later, after you've covered the interval material in Chapter 2, you can come back to Track 4 and sing through these exercises again using pitches.

Staccato Swing Eighth Notes

When jazz musicians want to perform **staccato swing eighth notes**, they treat the first eighth note as a short "Dit" and make the second eighth note a legato "duh." This results in a galloping rhythm as in "Dit-duh, Dit-duh, Dit," etc. In the following example, the text under the top line represents the straight eighth-note interpretation. Underneath that is the way it would be played using a swing-eighth feel.

Dit dit Dit dit Dit dit Dit dit　Doo　daht ___　　Doo Dit dit Doo Dit dah ___

Dit duh Dit duh Dit duh Dit duh Doo___ daht__　　Doo Dit duhDoo Dit duh ___

Of course there are times when straight staccato eighth notes may be desired in the middle of a swing phrase. If this happens, the words "straight" or "even" are usually added above the music to make the performance intention clear. If that had been the case for the previous example, a knowledgeable jazz musician would perform the top line for the first measure, then switch to the lower line for the second measure. Continuing on, they would then go back to the top line for the first three beats of measure 3, and return to the bottom line for beat 4 so that the anticipation of the C in measure 4 would still swing... Sound confusing? Don't worry; you'll probably never see anything like this unless you're performing something that is very experimental rhythmically.

As you move on to the next chapter, don't forget about what was said at the very beginning of this chapter. Musicians make mistakes reading music for two main reasons: 1) they don't recognize the way the music looks, which means they see symbols on the page, but don't know what the symbols actually mean; and 2) they haven't really mastered their instrument yet. Hopefully what has been presented here will help you address the first issue. And of course, only the time you're willing to put in to practice can address the second issue.

2 Hearing Intervals in the Major Scale

Comfortable Range

Before we begin our study of intervals we need to know something about you. This is the first part of a two-part question. What is the highest note you can sing comfortably? Notice the question didn't ask for the highest note you can sing; it added the word "comfortably." If we try to sing something high that puts a strain on our voice, we will often sing it flat. If we are trying to hear how a melody sounds, or arpeggiate the notes in a five- or six-note chord, or sing up and down the notes of a scale we're trying to get into our head, and if we are straining to hit the high notes, we're going to go out of tune rather quickly, or worse yet, start coughing because our throat begins itching from the strain. So let's ask that question again.

What is the highest note you can sing comfortably? You can either check yourself using your instrument or find a piano to do this. Most men can sing an E at the top of the treble clef staff. Women, who are singing one octave higher than men, can also sing E, whether they are an alto or soprano. Write your answer here.

The highest note you can sing comfortably is _____.

Now let's ask the next part of this question: What is the lowest note you can sing comfortably? In the case of low notes, if we go too low, we strain to hit the note we want and tend to go sharp in the process. You should be able to sing down at least one octave plus another fifth or sixth without any trouble. The average, untrained singer has a range of at least twelve notes (an octave and a half or so), while others can sing two octaves or more. Write your answer here.

The lowest note you can sing comfortably is _____.

Now you know your comfortable range for singing. Why is this important? The answer might surprise you. You don't have to sing something in the key it was written in order "hear it." For example, if you play a band instrument like saxophone, trumpet, or French horn, the note you hear when you play written C on your instrument is not concert C. Piano, flute, string instruments, and brass instruments like trombone and tuba play in concert keys, but the rest don't. Hearing concert C isn't as important as hearing a note and understanding how it relates to the other notes around it. For that you need to develop a good sense of relative pitch and you need a system for labeling and understanding what you hear—and the best way to do that is to learn to use the solfege system.

The Need for Solfege

There are many systems that have been developed over the years to help us improve our ability to hear music without having to use an instrument. Unfortunately, some musicians will tell you that all you need to do is use "la, la, la" or use your own made-up "scat" syllables to get through any particular passage you want to learn. The truth, however, is that with this way of thinking, everything becomes very imprecise and, when errors are made, it becomes almost impossible to recall where the error was made and how to fix it. It might be useful to compare this attitude to driving around in a strange town where all the streets have the same name ("la, la, la"), or discovering that even when you do find a street sign on one block, the name isn't the same on the next block (scat singing). In either case, when you get lost, you'll stay lost!

Other musicians will tell you that all you need is numbers. It's true that numbers are an improvement, but as soon as chromatic pitches are introduced, numbers become impossible to use because, depending on the situation, one number might need to serve for A♭ and A♮, or A♮ and A♯. Further, when the music modulates it becomes very difficult to determine exactly where and why it occurred.

Solfege is another approach that offers a number of advantages over both numbers and the "no-name" systems because it was created specifically to make reading and remembering music easier, not harder. The power of solfege only becomes apparent after you have had some experience with it. For now, let us simply say that students with an understanding of solfege will "feel differently" about a "DO" chord than they do about a "FA" chord even though both chords are "major" in quality. This is because to a person trained in solfege, a "DO" chord is at rest in a chord progression while a "FA" chord is not.

As presented here, solfege will: 1) help you to identify and practice the intervals and chords you have trouble hearing (and therefore probably don't use effectively); 2) will give you a systematic way to hear and organize the scales and modes used by jazz musicians as they solo; 3) will help you to sing through the melodies and chord progressions you encounter in jazz; and 4) will help you to recall chord progressions without the need for a keyboard instrument.

Diatonic Solfege

Most good musicians, whether they have studied solfege or not, are likely to know the solfege names for the major scale, so we'll begin with these names as a starting point. The solfege names DO, RE, MI, FA, SO, LA, TI, DO and DO, TI, LA, SO, FA, MI, RE, DO traditionally refer to the ascending and descending forms of the major scale. In order to save time, capital letters can be used to represent these names. Here are the diatonic notes of the B♭ major scale using letters.

Sing this scale aloud, but don't try to sing it in B♭. In other words, don't play B♭ on some instrument and then try to sing the scale "at pitch." It's not necessary. Just give yourself a fairly low note, one that's above your lowest note, and call it "DO." Sing up the scale and stop at the highest note in the scale. This note should be below your highest note and should be comfortable to sing. That's all you need to do to begin using solfege to improve your ability to hear music.

Learning Solfege Names Using the Major Scale

The notes of the major scale are a great place to begin because so many of the tunes we perform in jazz are based on that scale. The following block drill will help you get more familiar with the solfege names for the major scale. What is a "block drill"? Block drills are short practice routines found throughout the book, placed within a shaded box. They are intended to help you focus on recognizing and recalling intervals, scales, chords, patterns, and chord progressions without actually having to hear the notes themselves.

Block Drill: Solfege Names in the Major Scale

1. Give yourself a starting DO in the middle of your vocal range.

2. Sing a major scale up and down one octave (DRMFSLTD–DTLSFMRD).

3. Select a different note and call it DO.

4. Sing a major scale from that note up and down one octave (DRMFSLTD–DTLSFMRD).

5. Repeat steps one through four using many different starting notes.

When you can do this quickly and accurately in eighth notes at a moderate tempo, starting on any note that is comfortably within your vocal range, you have completed this drill.

Your drill should look something like this.

Give yourself a starting DO.

You may be wondering why we need to change keys so often. It's because most jazz tunes change keys several times before they finish. Some tunes change keys every two measures while others change keys after only two beats. Jazz soloists must start out thinking about soloing in one key and then immediately change to another key, just like the drill above. The advantage of knowing solfege helps us move out of one key and into the new key quickly and easily.

Shifting Octaves

You probably noticed that in doing the previous drill, certain keys were simply too high or too low to sing comfortably. This is why many jazz singers only want to sing tunes in unusual keys. It's not to make the tune hard for the instrumentalists; it's to make things more comfortable for their voices. Fortunately for our current studies, we are only singing up and down scales, so there's a way to handle that problem even in keys that would normally be too high or too low for us to sing easily. It's called "shifting octaves."

> **Block Drill: Shifting Octaves Down**
>
> Play the note B♭ on your instrument and call it DO. Sing up the major scale as far as you can go comfortably, then shift down an octave when you have gotten to a note that feels too high to sing. Continue to sing upwards. Each time you get near the top of your vocal range, shift down. Repeat this drill several times. Each time shift down using different notes near the top of your range.
>
> When you can do this quickly and accurately in eighth notes at a steady tempo, you have completed the drill.

If your top note is a C, your Block Drill might look something like this.

Now let's try shifting octaves while descending. If your top note is a C, your drill might look something like this.

D T L S F M R D T L S F M R D T L S F M R D T L S F M R D T L S

> ### Block Drill: Shifting Octaves Up
>
> Play the note B♭ on your instrument and call it DO. Sing down the major scale as far as you can go comfortably, then shift up an octave when you have gotten to a note that feels too low to sing. Continue to sing downwards. Each time you get near the bottom of your vocal range, shift up. Repeat this drill several times, each time shifting up using different notes.
>
> When you can do this quickly and accurately in eighth notes at a steady tempo, you have completed the drill.

Chromatic Names for Chromatic Notes

When chromatic or color notes are added to the major scale, new names are needed. Chromatic solfege uses specific names to relate these chromatic notes and all diatonic notes into a single twelve-note system. The example below uses C as the starting note, DO. Notice that chromatic names can be written out completely or written with a capital letter that includes either a slash (/) to indicate raised names or a backslash (\) to indicate lowered names. This is an excellent way to deal with chromatic solfege names quickly.

D DI R RI M F FI S SI L LI T D   D T TE L LE S SE F M ME R RA D

In this book we use the shorthand system of capital letters for our musical examples, but retain the full letter names when writing about them in the text.

As you can see in the previous example there are more than twelve possible names listed. This is because in the study of traditional solfege, chromatic names are intended to indicate the direction in which a melody is moving. The ascending chromatic names all end with "i" pronounced "ee," as in "tree" or "bee."

DI RI FI SI LI

Descending chromatic names usually end with "e" pronounced "ay," as in "tray" or "bay." However, there is one exception to this principle because the diatonic note RE already has the "ay" sound. In this case, the lowered chromatic name for flatted RE becomes RA pronounced "ah," as in "rah."

TE LE SE ME RA

Here's a block drill to help you become more familiar with chromatic solfege names in major keys.

> ### Block Drill: Learning Chromatic Solfege Names
>
> 1. Give yourself a starting note and sing through the following exercise several times until you are familiar with the chromatic names.
>
> 2. Skip around between different measures in the exercise and sing the chromatic names for whichever note you happen to land on.

There are actually more chromatic names possible, but they're more theoretical than practical—so we've left them out of this exercise. This is why you won't find notes like E♯, B♯, C♭, or F♭ on our list in the key of C major. They might be useful in some theoretical situations, but we favor using the names we are most likely to encounter as we read through a piece of music—and those notes are usually spelled to make reading easier, even when the spelling is wrong theoretically.

Now we're ready to begin a more detailed study of the intervals found in the major scale.

Interval Studies Using the Major Scale

Intervals sounded together are called harmonic, and when sounded successively are called melodic. Melodic intervals may ascend or descend. When an interval spans less than one octave, it is called simple, and when greater than one octave, it is referred to as compound.

Why should we be able to recognize intervals quickly? Recognizing intervals quickly helps us to hear and identify chord progressions, outline chords and scales, and hear or write down the melodies to tunes or improvisational ideas without needing to use a keyboard instrument to help us.

Minor Seconds and Major Sevenths

The smallest distance between two notes is the minor second, which also happens to be the smallest interval found in the major scale. All remaining intervals are built by adding minor seconds together until the desired size has been reached. In the major scale, the minor second occurs in two places, between MI–FA and TI–DO. In the C major scale, those notes would be as follows.

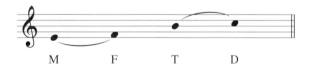

TI–DO says you're going home while MI–FA doesn't. FA–MI says you've arrived at the third of the key and DO–TI says you've just left home (DO).

If we shift the first note up an octave for each interval, we get a new interval, the major seventh.

Since the minor second and the major seventh are related this way, we can call them an interval pair. Interval pairs are two notes that are identical when any octaves present have been removed. The minor second interval is easy to sing, but this isn't the case with the major seventh. The intervals MI down to FA or FA up to MI are much harder to identify and sing. Likewise, TI down to DO or DO up to TI is also much harder to identify and sing. The following block drill will help you become more sensitive to where these intervals are located.

This how the first part of this block drill might look in the key of A major.

And this is how the first part of that drill might look with a few major sevenths added. Don't try to make all the intervals into major sevenths, just a few.

Interval Studies for Minor Seconds and Major Sevenths

The interval studies that follow are designed to help improve your ability to read and hear minor seconds and major sevenths quickly.

#1 in B♭

Here are some creative ways to practice this exercise.

1. Write in the solfege names under the notes and sing through the exercise from beginning to end until you can sing it accurately at a moderate tempo.

2. Begin somewhere in the middle of the exercise and sing through until you arrive back at your starting note. Do this several times.

#1 in B♭

3. Imagine the exercise in a meter such as 3/8 or 4/8 and sing it while placing accents on the downbeats of each imaginary measure. If the last measure doesn't have enough notes, sustain the note or end with a rest—make up your own rhythms.

Listen to how the first interval study might sound performed in 3/8, 4/8, and 5/8. Notice how the time signatures cause accents to fall in different places. As a result, something that's easy to feel rhythmically in 3/8 might become more difficult in 4/8, 5/8, or some other time signature.

TRACK 5
Exercises 1–3

Exercise 1 in 3/8

Of course, no one is requiring that you read this in 5/8. The point is to challenge yourself as much as possible; so if you like the idea, use it.

Practice each of the following interval studies to improve your ability to recognize minor second and major seventh intervals as you read.

#1 in B♭

#2 in B♭

#3 in A♭

#4 in A♭

#5 in F

#6 in D

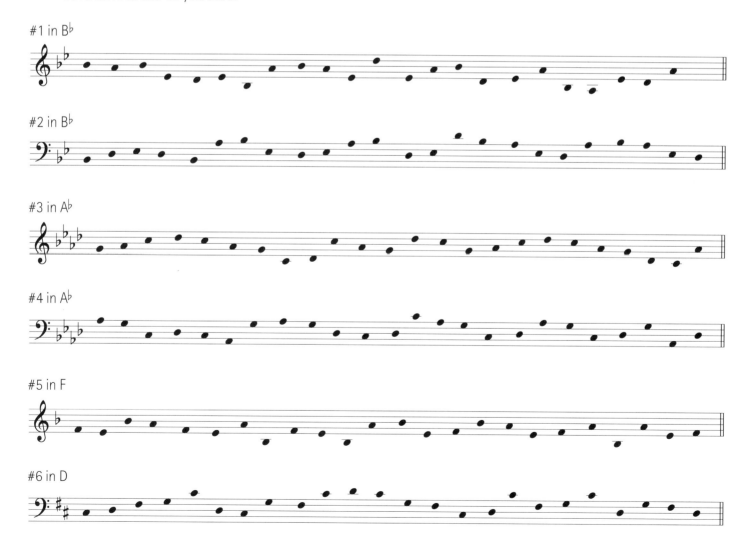

Major Seconds and Minor Sevenths

The next interval pair is the major second (equal to two minor seconds) and minor seventh. These intervals occur between DO–RE, RE–MI, FA–SO, SO–LA, and LA–TI. Here are the major second intervals in the C major scale.

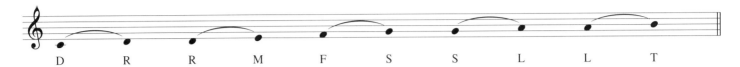

And here are the minor seventh intervals in C major.

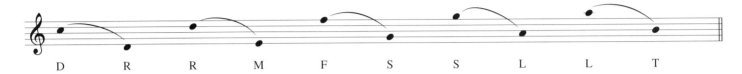

Just like in the previous exercise, major seconds are easy to sing and hear, while minor sevenths are much harder. Since all the notes of the major scale are present in these intervals, your goal is to try to sort out for yourself what makes each pair sound different.

Block Drill: Major Seconds and Minor Sevenths in the Major Scale

1. Give yourself a starting note (DO) and sing through the following patterns to get a feel for these intervals. Remember to pause for two beats before starting each new pattern. Start by focusing on major seconds.

    DRSF   MRSL   FSTL   LTRD   SLMR
    FSRD   LSRM   LTSF   RMLS   DRTL

2. Give yourself a new starting note (DO), start at a different place in the patterns and sing through them again.

3. Repeat step 2 many times until the drill is easy to do starting with any of the patterns.

When you can do this drill easily using major seconds, begin adding minor sevenths.

This how the first five measures of this block drill would look in the key of C major.

And this is how it would look with a few minor sevenths added.

Interval Studies for Major Seconds and Minor Sevenths

Next are some interval studies for mastering major seconds and minor sevenths, with a few major ninths thrown in for good measure. Major ninths are major seconds expanded by one octave, so they certainly belong here along with the other intervals.

#7 in C

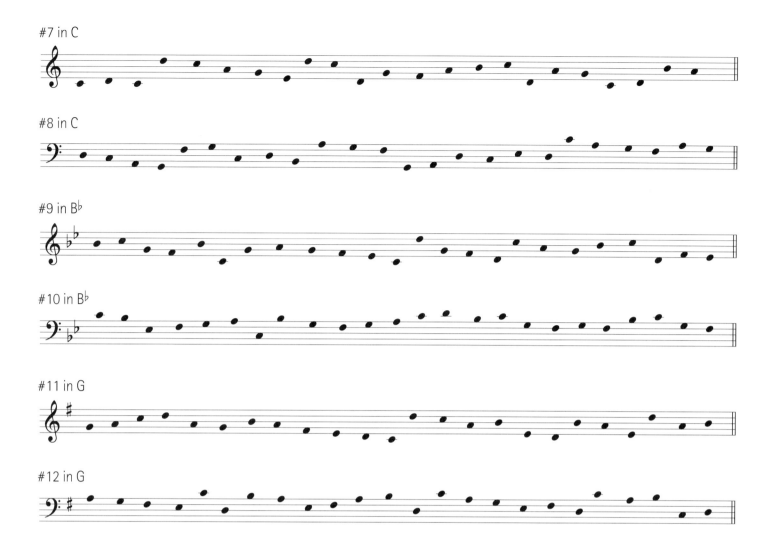

#8 in C

#9 in B♭

#10 in B♭

#11 in G

#12 in G

Dictation Exercises Using Major/Minor Seconds and Major/Minor Sevenths in F Major

The next exercise involves listening to the CD and figuring out the intervals you hear. All intervals are major/minor seconds or major/minor sevenths. The tonic note DO is played at the beginning of the exercise. Following the count-off, the interval is played as two quarter notes. You have two beats to figure out what the interval is using solfege syllables. Give your answer by singing the pitches you hear, two beats later, using solfege. If you are correct, you will end up singing in unison with the CD track, the correct solfege syllables. The following example outlines how the beginning of the track is constructed.

TRACK 6

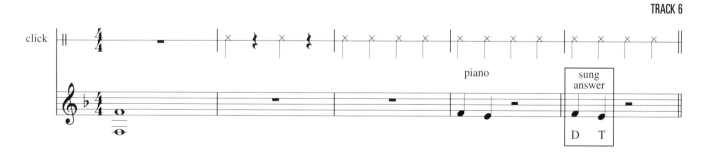

If you need extra time, pause the track and take a few moments to think about your answer. Also, it might be beneficial to play through the entire track once, with the right channel turned down so you don't hear any of the answers (the answer track is only on the right channel). You may then turn the right channel back up and try to sing along with the answer track. And you don't need to start from the beginning each time you want to practice. Just listen to the tonic note and then skip ahead several examples to begin at a new starting place. It becomes a brand new exercise.

These exercises use the same format as Track 6, but in the key of C major.

TRACK 7

Minor Thirds and Major Sixths

The next interval pair involves the minor third (three minor seconds) and the major sixth. These intervals occur between RE–FA, MI–SO, LA–DO, and TI–RE. Here are the notes for these minor third intervals in C major.

And here are the same notes shown as major sixths.

Minor thirds and major sixths give the music a sense of skipping around instead of just moving in steps. Most jazz soloists use a mix of intervals to create variety in their solos.

Block Drill: Minor Thirds and Major Sixths in the Major Scale

1. Give yourself a starting note (DO) and sing through the following patterns to get a feel for these intervals. Rest two beats between patterns. Start by focusing on minor thirds.

   DLFR MSTR LDRF TRSM
   RFLD RTSM SMTR DLFR

2. Give yourself a new starting note (DO), start at a different place in the patterns, and sing through them again.

3. Repeat step 2 many times until the drill is easy to do starting with any of the patterns.

When you can do this drill easily using minor thirds, begin adding major sixths.

This how the first four measures of this block drill would look in the key of A major.

And here are the first four measures using both minor thirds and major sixths.

Interval Studies for Minor Thirds and Major Sixths

As with the previous interval studies, work through the exercises using the three practice steps.

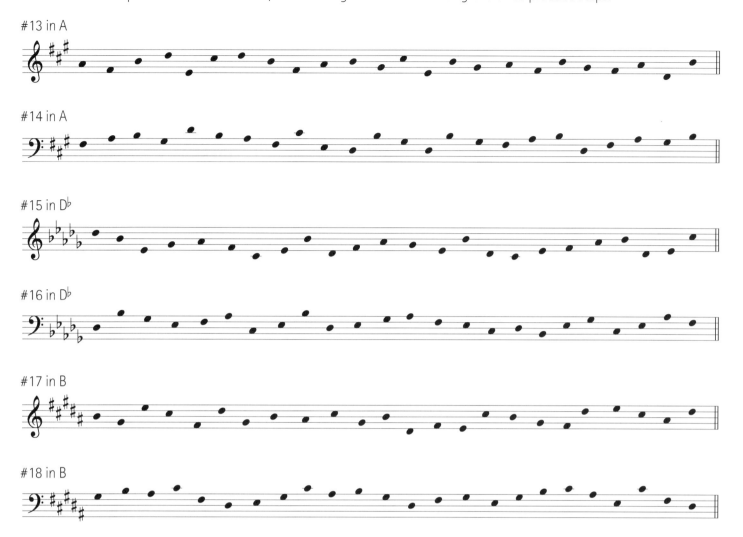

#13 in A

#14 in A

#15 in D♭

#16 in D♭

#17 in B

#18 in B

Major Thirds and Minor Sixths

The major third (four minor seconds) and minor sixth interval pairs are found in three places, between DO–MI, FA–LA, and SO–TI.

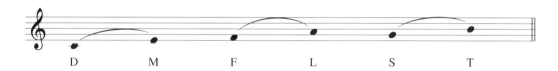

D   M   F   L   S   T

Here are the same notes shown as minor sixths.

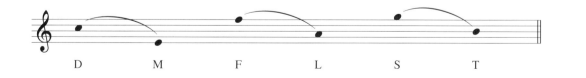

D   M   F   L   S   T

Like minor thirds and major sixths, these intervals are used to give the music a sense of skipping around. They are also used (in combination with minor thirds) to create all the commonly used triads and seventh chords found in jazz, so being familiar with them makes chord recognition much faster.

Block Drill: Major Thirds and Minor Sixths in the Major Scale

1. Give yourself a starting note (DO) and sing through the following patterns. Rest two beats between patterns. Focus on major thirds at first.

    DMLF   STMD   FLTS

    MDTS   FLDM   STLF

2. Give yourself a new starting note (DO), start at a different place in the patterns, and sing through them again.

3. Repeat step 2 many times until the drill is easy to do starting with any of the patterns.

When you can do this drill easily using major thirds, begin adding minor sixths.

This how the first three measures of this block drill would look in the key of C major.

And here are the first two measures using both major thirds and minor sixths.

Interval Studies for Major Thirds and Minor Sixths

Again, work through the exercises using the three practice steps.

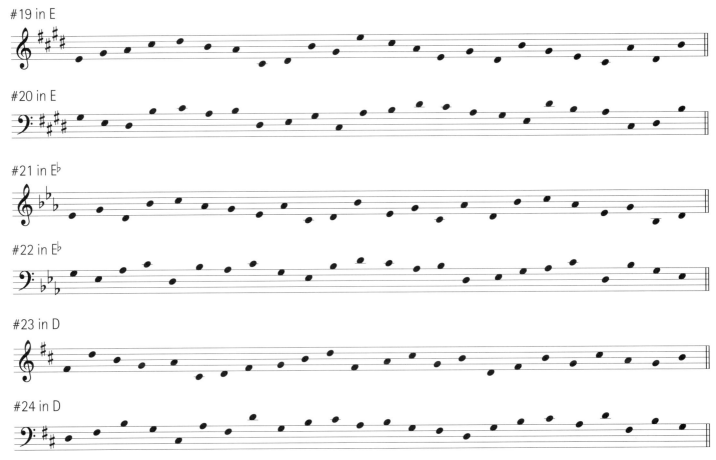

Dictation Exercises Using Major/Minor Thirds and Major/Minor Sixths

The exercises on Track 8 use the same format found in the previous dictation exercises (see Tracks 6 and 7). **TRACK 8**

Perfect Fourths and Perfect Fifths

Perfect fourths and perfect fifths are among the most common intervals heard in chord progressions. Yet many musicians have difficulties with this interval pair because they sound so similar to each other. There are several places in the major scale where these intervals can be found. They occur between DO–FA, RE–SO, MI–LA, SO–DO, LA–RE, and TI–MI. The following shows where they are located in C major as perfect fourths.

Here are the perfect fifth intervals in C major.

Block Drill: Perfect Fourths and Perfect Fifths in the Major Scale

1. Give yourself a starting note (DO) and sing through the following patterns. Rest two beats between patterns. Because of the wide skips found in both intervals, it is better to begin combining perfect fourths and perfect fifths right away.

   DFRS   MLSD   LRTM   SRFD   MTRL   DSLM
   FDSR   LMDS   RLMT   RSDF   TMLR   SDML

2. Give yourself a new starting note (DO), start at a different place in the patterns, and sing through them again.

3. Repeat step 2 many times until the drill is easy to do starting with any of the patterns.

This is how the beginning of this block drill would look in the key of G major. Some of the intervals are perfect fourths and others are perfect fifths.

Interval Studies for Perfect Fourths and Perfect Fifths

As before, practice using the three steps.

#25 in F

#26 in F

#27 in G

#28 in G

#29 in A

#30 in A

The Tritone

The final interval to be studied in this chapter is the **tritone**: an unusual interval that is sometimes called an **augmented fourth** and other times a **diminished fifth**. In the key of C major, the tritone notes are FA and TI. FA up to TI is an augmented fourth. FA down to TI is a diminished fifth. Either way they both equal three whole-steps, which is where the name "tritone" comes from.

F   T   F   T

The tritone is unstable because its notes want to expand or contract, but they don't like to be left alone. Normally TI wants to go up to DO and FA wants to go down to MI. What's interesting is we've actually practiced this interval earlier in this chapter when we were working on the block drill "Minor Seconds and Major Sevenths in the Major Scale." If you go back and look at that material, you will see the tritone operating in the major scale. At that time you were focused on hearing minor seconds and major sevenths. Practice that block drill again, but focus on the tritone notes FA and TI. You should immediately begin to hear how those notes typically move within the major scale.

Interval Studies for Tritones

While it is true that you have already been studying tritones while working on the natural resolution of minor seconds and major sevenths, tritones aren't required melodically to resolve by half steps. They can appear and then move or jump around in unusual ways. For that reason, the following interval studies are also unusual because the tritones don't always resolve to where they would be expected to in traditional situations such as TI–DO or FA–MI.

#31 in C

#32 in F

#33 in G

#34 in B♭

#35 in A♭

#36 in A

Dictation Exercises Using Perfect Fourths and Fifths and Tritones

The exercises on Track 9 use the same format found in the previous dictation exercises (Tracks 6, 7, and 8).   **TRACK 9**

Associating Intervals with Tunes

There is a long-standing tradition of associating intervals with tunes. In some cases, just remembering the lyrics to a particular tune will allow you to recall it. For example, the words "Happy Birthday to You" immediately allow us to recall the melody and the interval of an ascending major second found at the beginning of the song. As you can see, this actually does work, although it is not particularly useful unless the tunes recalled are truly familiar to the person using the technique. By extension, this can be a method for recalling types of chords and even inversions.

The following is a list of tunes you can use to start developing a tune/interval list for yourself. But remember, the list is of no use unless you can easily recall the tunes. It must be *your* list if it is to work for you. If there are songs or tunes on the list that you don't know, replace them with ones you *do* know.

Complete the following list of tunes. You will need to identify, and write in, at least one melody or phrase from a tune that you can easily recall for each interval within a range of one octave in both directions. It doesn't matter how sophisticated the melody is, as long as you can easily recall it. If you don't have a tune in mind for a particular interval, consult any good fake book for the tunes suggested.

Tune/Interval List

INTERVAL	POSSIBLE TUNE	YOUR CHOICE(S)
Ascending Minor 2nd	I Could Write a Book What's New?	_____
Descending Minor 2nd	Mood Indigo Stella by Starlight	_____
Ascending Major 2nd	Bluesette I Got Rhythm	_____
Descending Major 2nd	Satin Doll Honeysuckle Rose	_____
Ascending Minor 3rd	Cherokee Perdido	_____
Descending Minor 3rd	Misty Dixie	_____
Ascending Major 3rd	I Can't Get Started When the Saints Go Marching In	_____
Descending Major 3rd	Summertime In a Mellow Tone	_____
Ascending Perfect 4th	All the Things You Are When I Fall in Love	_____
Descending Perfect 4th	Our Day Will Come All of Me	_____
Diminished 5th	The Simpsons Theme Blue Seven	_____
Ascending Perfect 5th	My Favorite Things Star Wars Theme	_____
Descending Perfect 5th	It Don't Mean a Thing Feelings	_____
Ascending Minor 6th	Theme for Carnival Sunny	_____
Descending Minor 6th	Love Story	_____
Ascending Major 6th	Days of Wine and Roses Take the "A" Train	_____
Descending Major 6th	Nobody Knows the Trouble I've Seen Over There	_____
Ascending Minor 7th	I'll Close My Eyes Somewhere (from *West Side Story*)	_____
Descending Minor 7th	Watermelon Man	_____
Ascending Major 7th	Ceora	_____
Descending Major 7th	I Love You	_____
Ascending Octave	Blue Bossa	_____
Descending Octave	Willow Weep for Me	_____

3 Hearing Melodies in Major

The next logical step after learning intervals is to examine melodies. For the jazz musician, learning a melody means many things: 1) it's a tune or theme intended to be changed and reinterpreted every time it's performed; 2) it's an ensemble part that needs to be performed consistently each time an arrangement is played; or 3) it's a resource for motivic and melodic ideas for use in soloing.

Some melodies have a vocal character—they have a relatively narrow range, tend not to modulate very much, aren't very complex rhythmically, and are generally diatonic. Others have an instrumental character—they have a wider range, contain rhythmically complex or very dense passages full of triplets and sixteenth notes, modulate frequently (and often in an abrupt manner), and are intended to be performed with an instrument other than the voice. Not surprisingly, melodies with an instrumental character generally don't have words because they are not intended to be sung.

Three Basic Steps to Hearing Short Melodic Phrases

Regardless of whether melodies are vocal or instrumental in character we go about learning them the same way. The process usually begins as we scan through a piece of music and come across a few phrases that look unusual or challenging. This could happen as we look through a new band arrangement, or we might just be looking through a book of tunes, see one that looks interesting and wonder how it sounds. When that happens, applying the following steps can help us solve many of the problems in hearing the music.

Step 1

Sing through the phrase as a rhythm exercise. As you do, look for any unusual rhythms or jazz articulations that might be present and work them out. If necessary, write the rhythm syllables under the notes, then chant the phrase on one note. Remember, pitches aren't important at this point—rhythms and articulations *are*.

Step 2

Look for the highest and lowest notes in each phrase so you can figure out a comfortable range for singing, and give yourself a starting DO for reference. Sing through the notes very slowly, out of tempo, using solfege. In other words, treat the notes as a string of intervals. Pay careful attention to any awkward skips that are present. When you can sing the intervals correctly, move on to the third and final step.

Step 3

At this point you know how the rhythms and articulations sound, and also how the pitches sound. It's time to combine the rhythms and jazz articulations with the correct pitches. When you do this it will sound very similar to what jazz vocalists do when they scat sing, but it differs in one important aspect: you are using the rhythm syllables and jazz articulations as lyrics, they aren't being made up spontaneously. For this reason you will be able to recall the phrases later in much the same way you recall the melody to "Happy Birthday to You" simply by thinking about the lyrics. Here's an example: "Doo duh Doo dut -- duh---, duh--Doo dut" is the way most jazz musicians would perform the following phrase in the style of a famous Duke Ellington tune. Even though there are actual words to this song, think of these syllables and you can easily recall the tune.

Doo duh Doo dut   duh   duh   Doo dut

Can you hear and remember this tune using the syllables? If so, then the rhythm syllables became the lyrics.

The following melodic phrases give you a chance to apply what's been covered in the first three chapters to reading and hearing jazz phrases: 1) look them over rhythmically, chanting them on one pitch; 2) sing through the notes as a string of intervals; and 3) put it all together, singing the melodies using the rhythmic syllables. Remember that you don't need to sing these phrases in the key in which they are written. Pick a key that works for you rather than trying to strain for high or low notes. All these phrases have a range of one octave or less. Tracks 10 and 11 play Exercises 1–4.

TRACK 10
Swing feel

TRACK 11
Straight feel

Exercise 1

Exercise 2

Exercise 3

Exercise 4

Exercise 5

Exercise 6

Exercise 7

Exercise 8

Exercise 9

Exercise 10

Exercise 11

Exercise 12

Jazz Melodies and Articulations: Swing Feel and Straight Feel

On the CD, the first four phrases are demonstrated with a voice accompanied by a drum kit. Track 10 plays the exercises with a swing feel and Track 11 plays them with a straight feel. The remaining phrases are there for you to practice on your own; they include only the drum part on the CD. As a reminder, the first four phrases are not performed in the keys in which they are written. Notice that before each melody the singer gives himself a starting note as a reference pitch, then sings the phrase in that key. Listen to or sing along with the first four tracks, then pick a key for each remaining exercise and sing them on your own along with the drum tracks.

Here are twelve more phrases for you to practice. You can use Tracks 10 and 11 to accompany these phrases as well. Just turn down the volume on the voice track, give yourself a starting note, and sing along with the drum kit.

Exercise 13

Exercise 14

Exercise 15

Exercise 16

Exercise 17

Exercise 18

Exercise 19

Exercise 20

Exercise 21

Exercise 22

Exercise 23

Exercise 24

We will take up similar material when we study melodies in minor keys later in the book. An excellent resource for singing jazz phrases is transcriptions of solos. In particular, transcriptions of trumpet solos are useful because they usually don't cover the wide range found in sax solos or piano solos.

4 Hearing Root Movements in Major

Analyzing Chord Progressions

Before we begin we need to point out that if you have no background in analyzing chord progressions, you should get a music theory book and work on your analytical skills before going on to the following material. We will be presenting some of the basics on chord analysis and chord progressions, but you will get more out of it if you already have some understanding of Roman numeral usage in harmonic analysis.

The following shows a list of chords commonly found in the major scale. Below each chord is a staff with the root pitch and the chord's basic qualities spelled out in rhythm. (The purpose of the rhythm in the root-movement line will be demonstrated later.)

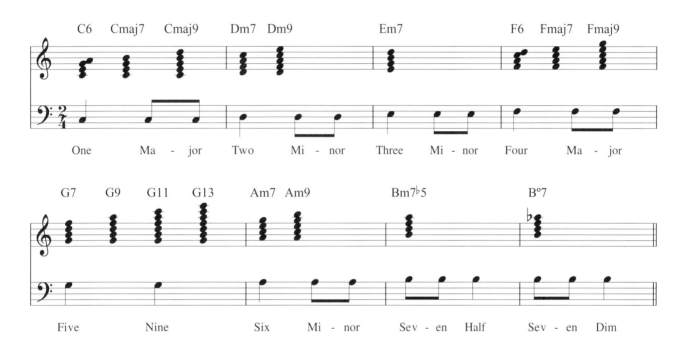

All of these chords have at least four notes, some have five, and the G13 chord has seven different notes. Yet in each case, there is only one name needed to define each chord. Let's begin our explanation by looking at the V chord and vii chord.

Calling V Chords "Five Nine"

V chords (or V7: "dominant seventh") are the only diatonic chords that consist of a major triad and a minor seventh. This is what makes them different from I chords and IV chords, which normally add major sixths or major sevenths as the fourth note. In jazz, and for discussions in this book, we will consider and refer to all V chords as "Five Nine," even though the V7 (G7 in C major) doesn't necessarily have a ninth present.

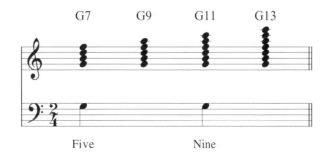

Now it might seem strange to call this chord "Five Nine" instead of "Five Seven," but there's a practical reason for doing so. If we call the V chord "Five Seven," we aren't telling ourselves everything we need to know about the chord. V chords often appear with ninths, elevenths, and thirteenths added to them which have been altered in some way, so they aren't diatonic to the major key or major scale. If jazz musicians know a V chord has been altered, they know that melodic ideas taken only from the major scale probably won't be satisfactory for soloing. There will be just too many notes that clash with the altered notes in the V chord. Over time, jazz musicians have come to call unaltered V chords "Five Nine," and to assume that this chord and its extensions are diatonic—unaltered. Therefore, we will use "Five Nine" for any and all unaltered V chords (i.e., V7, V9, V11, V13). It will save confusion later and avoid having a piano player ask "Are there any alterations?" if you say "This chord is a Five Seven chord."

Calling Chords "Seven Half" or "Seven Dim"

The diatonic vii chord in major is a minor seventh chord with flatted fifth. It's normally called a half-diminished seventh chord. The second example below is the chromatic vii chord. This is referred to simply as the diminished seventh chord, or as the "fully diminished" seventh chord. Both chords have diminished triads (TI–RE–FA), but different sevenths. The seventh of the half diminished chord is a minor seventh, which is why we call the chord half diminished. The seventh of the diminished is actually a diminished seventh, hence the name.

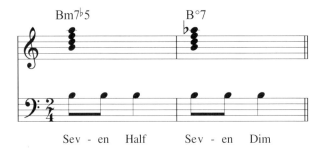

Below we see the pitches of the half diminished and diminished chords labeled with their solfege names.

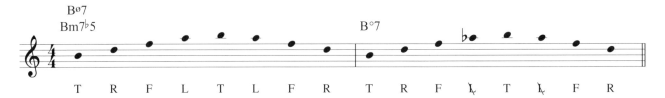

Note that the solfege names for the seventh in the diminished chord are written as LE for both ascending and descending directions. This is because we want to think of LE as a chord tone, not a melody note, and doing it this way eliminates confusing melodic and harmonic ideas. If LE weren't a chord tone, we would treat it melodically.

In major keys the diminished seventh chord is much more common than the half-diminished seventh chord. This doesn't mean half-diminished chords aren't useful, just that they're more likely to appear in minor keys than in major keys. We plan to take up the half-diminished chord in more detail when we study root movements in minor keys, but for now, we will assume the vii chord is fully diminished.

How do we name this chord? Saying the entire word "diminished" is awkward because there are so many syllables. We need something we can sing easily, so the abbreviation "Dim" is our choice. Whenever you see a vii chord in a chord progression, just call it "Seven Dim" if it's a diminished seventh chord.

Lead Sheets

Jazz music makes use of lead sheets and chord charts. A lead sheet contains the melody plus the chord symbols for a particular tune. A chord chart contains the name of the tune and the chord symbols—that's about all. The following example shows the first eight measures of the lead sheet to "A Rhythm Thing," a tune based on a chord progression in the style of George Gershwin. Use the three basic steps to hearing short melodic phrases presented in Chapter 3: 1) sing through the melody as a rhythm exercise; 2) find a comfortable range by looking for the highest and lowest notes and sing through the notes very slowly, out of tempo as a string of intervals using solfege; and 3) sing the melody as written.

A Rhythm Thing

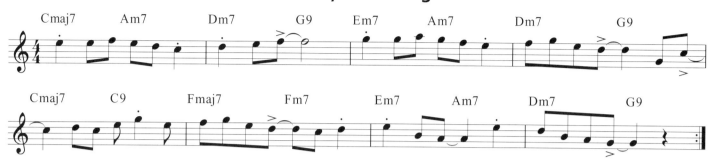

Singing Root Movements in Major

Now that you know what the melody sounds like, it's time to move on to the chord progression. The following steps, when applied carefully, will show you how to learn to hear any root movement you want, without having to play it.

Step 1

Sing through the letter names of the chord roots as a string of intervals. It doesn't matter which direction you go. The goal is to figure out how to move from root to root easily.

Step 2

Analyze the progression using Roman numerals and chord qualities. You should include the qualities in your analysis. This will remind you which chords are major, minor, or something else, which will become more important later when we start to explore chromatic chords.

Step 3

Sing through the root progression as you name the Roman numerals and chord qualities (write these out as needed).

Let's apply those steps to "A Rhythm Thing." The analysis is written under the lead on the first staff. On the CD, the chord progression is played through twice, with keyboard, bass, and drums. The voice sings on the first time through only. Listen to the track and sing along. Remember to focus on your root movements and not get distracted by the bass because the bass won't always be playing what you're singing. Good bass players create their own bass lines, and they're often wonderfully different from what's asked for by the roots of the chords. Fortunately, in progressions like this, bass players frequently play the root of each chord first before moving off on their own.

TRACK 12

As you can see, we sing the names for the chords in rhythm using Roman numerals. Now some people might ask "Why use Roman numeral names? Why not use the chord letter names instead?" The answer is that Roman numeral names tell us about relationships. For example, the first part of this progression is I–vi–ii–V. It doesn't matter what key we're in, "I–vi–ii–V" is a formula we can recognize and recall easily. If we used chord letter names we'd have twelve different keys to think about—we might not recognize the formula because there are just too many chords to remember. Think about It. Do you want to remember one "I–vi–ii–V" formula or forty-eight chord symbols?

The next example shows another progression, one that descends and uses a vii° chord. The chord progression is played through twice by keyboard, bass, and Brazilian-style drums. Listen to the track, sing along, then turn off the voice track and sing it by yourself.

TRACK 13

Hearing Chromatic Root Movements

Chromatic root movements occur when: 1) a diatonic chord is altered; or 2) when a chord is borrowed from another key. The most commonly altered or borrowed chord is the V chord (from a different key, i.e., in the key of C, using the V chord from the key of D, etc.), which is called a secondary dominant.

When a V chord moves up a perfect fourth or down a perfect fifth to a I chord (the SO-DO relationship), we say that the I chord has been tonicized. This is the most powerful root movement in music. The only place this can occur in a diatonic progression is between V-I. However, it's possible to tonicize any note we want by putting a secondary dominant in front of it. When that takes place, the note being tonicized acts like a tonic for part of the progression, hence the name.

To understand more about how secondary dominants work, it's useful to examine the circle of fifths.

The Circle of Fifths

By moving up five scale steps from any note (or one position clockwise on the circle of fifths), we come to the dominant for that key. Start on C, move five steps up the scale from C (DO–RE–MI–FA–SO), and you arrive at G, the root of the dominant (V chord) of C. Start on any other note and repeat the process and you arrive at the same place, the fifth note of that key.

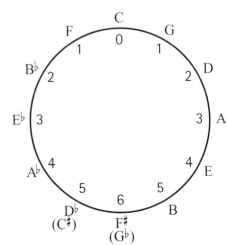

Another way of thinking about this is to move down (or one position counterclockwise on the circle). Start on C, think of it as the root of a dominant chord and count down five scale steps (SO–FA–MI–RE– DO) and you will arrive at F. Start on any other note and repeat the process; each time the note you start from will be SO, and you will arrive at DO.

Getting back to our discussion of secondary dominants, we now know that they always function as V chords of something, even though they aren't V of I. All we need to do to identify them as dominant chords when they occur is place the number "9" after the Roman numeral.

Let's take the chord progression to "A Rhythm Thing" and modify it using some secondary dominants. Some have diatonic root names, others have chromatic root names, but they are all secondary dominants. On the CD, the chord progression is played through twice by keyboard, bass, and drums, with the voice part on the first time only. On the recording, a I chord has been added after the last measure to finalize the progression.

A Rhythm Thing
(with diatonic and chromatic secondary dominants)

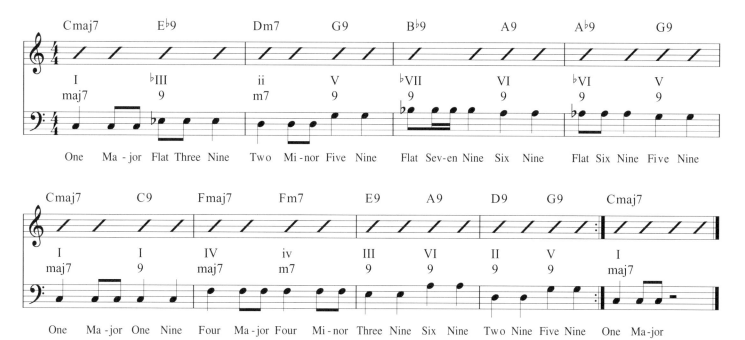

As you can see, the chromatic E♭9 and A♭9 chords required us to change the rhythms slightly in order to fit the names into two beats, but other than that, everything works in the same way as with diatonic dominants.

It's important to remember that while the secondary dominant is around, you're really not in the home key any longer, you're in the key the secondary dominant is tonicizing. Jazz players know that if they stay in the home key when they encounter a secondary dominant, many of the notes they play could sound wrong to their ears. So, just as they need to change, we need to change too.

Chromatic Diminished Sevenths

After secondary dominants, the next most common chromatic chords found in jazz progressions are chromatic diminished seventh chords. Chromatic diminished seventh chords should be thought of as vii chords borrowed from some other key. Normally these chords ascend, but you will find they can appear in any situation, ascending, descending or remaining stationary.

Next we have a chord progression to "You're in My Thoughts." It uses both chromatic diminished seventh chords and secondary dominants. The chord progression is played through twice, by keyboard, bass, and drums. The voice part sings on the first time only. Listen to the track, then sing along.

You're in My Thoughts

TRACK 15

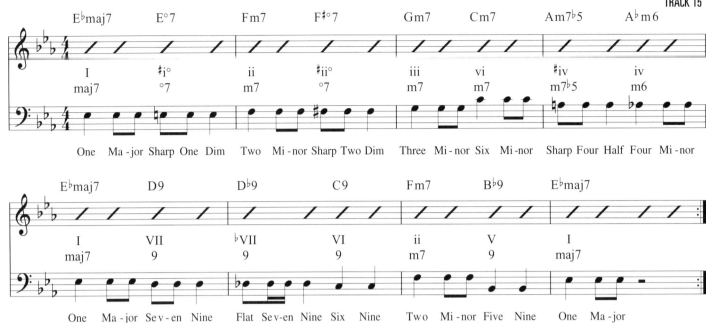

The first two measures contain two very common secondary diminished chords, the #i°7 and #ii°7. Both chords act as vii°7 chords. #i°7 acts like the vii°7 of ii and #ii°7 acts like the vii°7 of iii. The roots of both chords are also chromatic in the key of E major. They exert a very powerful pull upward which is in contrast to chromatic secondary dominants that tend to pull downward, as in measures 5–8, where D9 and D♭9 pull downward.

Augmented Chords

Augmented chords are usually I, IV, or V chords that have been altered. If we come across an augmented I chord or IV chord, we use the words "One Major Plus" or "Four Major Plus." "Major" tells us the quality of the third and "plus" tells us that the fifth has been raised. No matter what kind of chord is indicated, "plus" means #5, or augmented fifth.

Normally the augmented chord in jazz is a V9+. For this chord we say "Five Nine" to show that it's a dominant chord, then add the word "plus" to show that it's augmented, becoming "Five Nine Plus."

The next example features a short progression that shows an augmented I chord and an augmented V chord. The progression is played through twice, with the voice part on the first time only. Listen to the track, then sing along.

TRACK 16

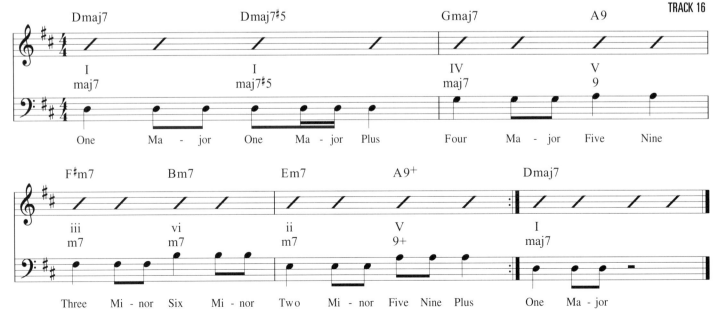

Hearing Secondary ii–V Progressions

As long as a secondary V chord stands alone, we label it within the key—II9, III9, etc. But when a secondary V chord is preceded by its own ii chord, it's treated a little differently. The combination of a ii chord followed by a V chord is another example of tonicization and implies that, for a moment, a new key is in effect. To show that this ii–V is from another key we call the new ii chord "Two of ___." The minute we add "of" to our analysis, we are saying this chord and the V chord that follows are related to each other, but not to the normal I chord. For example, if we see "Two of Two" it means the first chord is acting like a ii chord of the temporarily tonicized ii chord.

In this next progression in the key of F major, the ii chord is G. If this G chord were temporarily tonicized, an A minor chord would act as the ii of this G chord, as it is labeled in the second measure. The D chord functions as the V of the G chord, producing a ii–V progression.

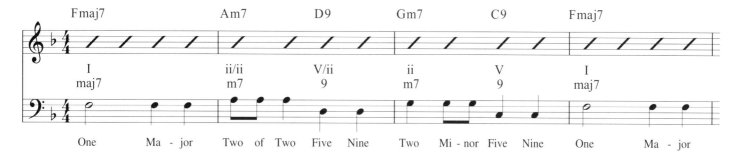

This should start to make more sense after we look at the next example. We call the next progression the "circle sequence" because not only does it demonstrate secondary ii–V progressions, but starting with the second measure, seven of the roots move counterclockwise around the circle of fifths, in order, from E all the way to B♭. It then drops down a half step and starts another sequence around the circle from A to F. The first ii–V in measure 2 is a ii–V of D, which is the sixth note in the key of F. Measure 3 contains a ii–V of C. Measure 4 is a ii–V of B♭. Measure 6 is a ii–V of G, and measure 7 is the ii–V in the home key of F.

On the CD, the progression is played through twice. Listen to the track, and then sing along.

The Circle Sequence

TRACK 17

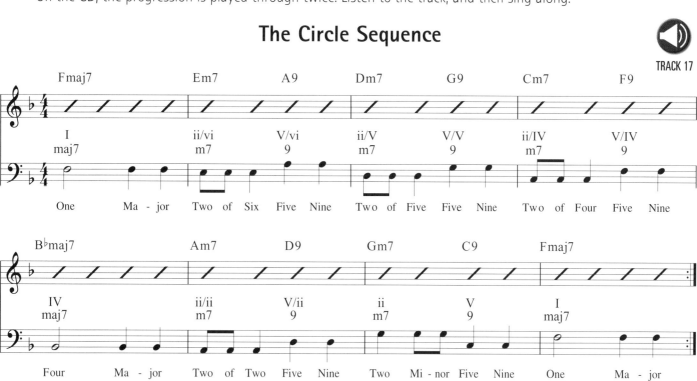

By now it should be very clear that you need to look for secondary ii–V formulas whenever you analyze a progression. You'll find a lot of them in popular jazz tunes.

Hearing Modulations

Modulations are similar to secondary ii–V progressions, but they differ in one important aspect: they stay in the secondary key for a while longer before returning home. When this happens we use "in" instead of "of" to announce that a modulation has taken place. Once we've called a chord "Two in," or "Five in," or even "One in" we've indicated a modulation. Everything from that point on is "in" the new key until we want to leave for another key or return to the home key.

In the following example, the "Two in Three" in the second measure says we're going from the key of F to the key of A, the third note in the key of F. In measure 6, the "Two in One" says it's time for us to return to F. Listen to the track, then sing through the second time, or eliminate the voice track and sing through both times.

TRACK 18

The difference between labeling something as a secondary ii–V or an actual modulation comes down to calling the chord "Two of" something in secondary modulations and "Two in" something in actual modulations. Also notice that in the actual modulation, we only use the word "in" for the first chord in the new key. After that, all chords are labeled as they function in the new key until another modulation occurs. This labeling system invokes only a simple difference between secondary and actual modulations, but sends a powerful message.

Modulation in Bridge Sections

Oftentimes modulations are saved for the bridge, or B sections, of thirty-two-measure AABA tunes. When this happens, the composer wants to leave the home key for a while and then work back to the home key by the end of the bridge.

The next example shows a bridge that does just that. This section begins in F major, but the actual beginning of the tune (not shown here) is in C major. Thus the bridge works its way back to the home key, ending on G9, the dominant of the C major A section. The Fmaj7 that begins the bridge is a chord that normally functions as a IV chord in C, and so we're going to call the F chord "One in Four Major" to show that we're modulating to F major for the first four measures of the bridge. Fmaj7 and B♭maj7 are the I and IV chords in F major.

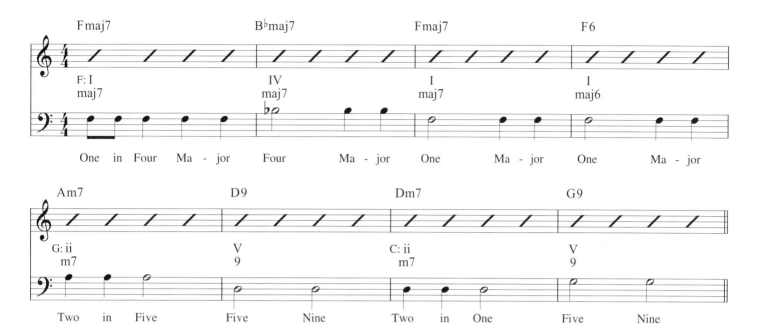

In measures 5–6, a secondary ii–V appears, but because each chord lasts a whole measure, they're around too long to be thought of as just a simple ii-V. In this case we're going to call the Am7 "Two in Five." This tells us we're leaving F major and we're headed for G. And notice that when we label a new modulation, we always do so in reference to the original key. Thus in this case, the Am7 chord is seen as a ii in G, which is V of the original key of C. The last two measures return to C major, so we call the Dm7 "Two in One." The minute we do that, we're confirming that we're back home in C major, just in time to start the last eight measures of the tune in the original key.

At this point you're probably still wondering why we treated what looked like a secondary ii–V (Am7–D9) as a modulation. The first part of our answer lies in the fact that even at a moderately fast tempo, we're spending a lot of time in the key of G major. We're there too long to think of these measures as being in the key of F. The other part of the answer lies in how most good jazz soloists would treat this moment in the bridge—they would tell you to solo in the key of G at this point. So if these two chords are around for a while and look like they're in G, and experienced soloists treat them that way, what else are you going to call it?

This covers most of the more common root-movement formulas you will run into in major keys. You should be able to sing the root movements to almost any chord progression you want using this method. Next we'll move on to how to hear and outline the chord qualities of the chord progressions themselves.

5 Hearing and Outlining Chords in Major

The material in this chapter is all about singing through chord progressions using a unique system of chord arpeggiation we refer to as "outlining." We use the term "outlining" rather than the traditional term "arpeggiation" because it describes what we're doing without carrying any preconceived notions. Hopefully as we go through this chapter, the things that make outlining special will become clear to you. Now let's make a quick review of music theory as it applies to diatonic chords in major keys.

Diatonic Chords

Chords are created when three or more notes are sounded simultaneously. In jazz, chords are most often built by combining thirds, although contemporary practice also finds chords built in fourths and seconds. The three most common three-note chords, called triads, are major, minor, and diminished. Because they are all found in the major scale, we refer to them as diatonic. This should make it easy as all we have to do is think of the solfege names for them, locate them in the major scale, and then sing them. Let's start with the major triad.

Major Triads

The major triad is built from two intervals, a major third and a minor third. In the major scale we can build major triads by taking five consecutive scale steps up from DO, FA, or SO, and singing only the first, third, and fifth notes. When a chord is identified by a capital letter, it's assumed to be a major chord. Here are the major triads found in the C major scale.

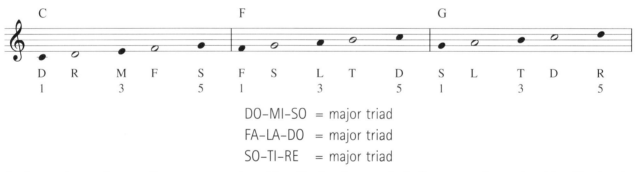

DO–MI–SO = major triad
FA–LA–DO = major triad
SO–TI–RE = major triad

Earlier we learned to use Roman numerals to identify chord roots. A similar system is used to identify chord qualities as well. The major chord starting with DO is the I chord, or tonic. The major chord starting with FA is the IV chord, or subdominant; and the major chord starting with SO is the V chord, or dominant.

Did you know that it's possible to outline one of the best-known chord progressions in jazz—the basic blues progression—using only these three chords? Track 19 plays the following example twice. The first time, the root-movement line is sung. The second time, the outlined chords are sung.

Basic Blues in C

TRACK 19

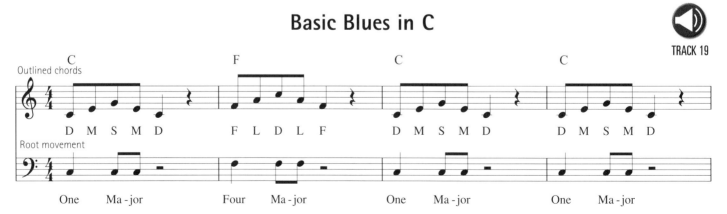

Almost all the blues progressions we use today come from blues progressions similar to this one, which became popular during the first half of the twentieth century. Of course, the point being made here is that in using only the tonic, subdominant, and dominant chords, it is possible to create and outline actual chord progressions.

Minor Triads

The minor triad is a three-note chord with the minor third on the bottom and the major third on top. To indicate a minor chord, the capital letter is followed by one of the following symbols: a lower-case "m," "mi," "min," or the minus sign "−."

Minor triads can be found starting from RE, MI, and LA in the major scale. We build the minor triad the same way we build the major triad. We start from the first note, skip the next, sing the third note, skip the fourth note and sing the fifth note. The first note of the ii chord is RE, the first note of the iii chord is MI, and the first note of the vi chord is LA.

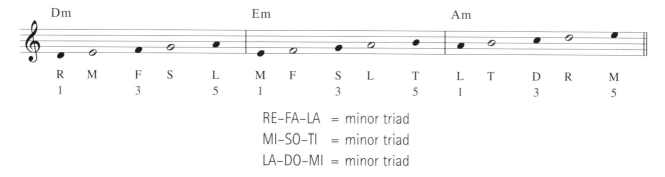

RE–FA–LA = minor triad
MI–SO–TI = minor triad
LA–DO–MI = minor triad

Diminished Triads

The diminished triad is a three-note chord built from two minor thirds. There's only one place a diminished triad can be found in the major scale, starting from TI. Sing TI, skip DO, sing RE, skip MI, and sing FA. The diminished symbol is often written as "dim" or "°."

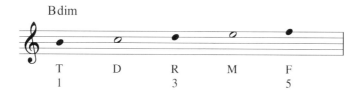

The next progression descends using the vii chord. The range spans one octave, and SO is the lowest note in the example. To find a good starting note sing up the scale from SO to SO to see if the octave you have selected feels okay. When you have this figured out, sing through the root movement and then sing the outline of the chord progression.

Triads Are All We Need

If you sang through the previous exercise, you probably found it was easy to do. But you are probably wondering: "What about extensions? Most jazz chords have extensions added to them. How do we deal with them?" You might be surprised by the answer. Once we know the notes of the basic triads and assign them their correct solfege names, that's all we need in order to hear a chord progression in our heads. In other words, all the diatonic extensions are implied, even if we don't sing or outline them.

To see what we mean, look at the following example, which shows four possible diatonic I chords found in a major key. In this case we're using the I chord in the key of C, but this applies, across the board, to any I chord in any key.

If we sing DO–MI–SO we know everything about these chords we need to know. We know they are all I chords because they start with DO, the first note of the major scale. We also know the chord quality is major. As long as we add only diatonic extensions like the major sixth, major seventh, or major ninth, nothing really changes—the chord is still just a I chord. Yes, it gets "thickened" a little, but that's all—it's still a I chord. The same thing would be true if we added diatonic extensions to any of the other chords. Try it for yourself, if you like. The simple truth is that diatonic extensions added to diatonic chords don't change anything! That's why we only need triads to outline most chord progressions even when extensions are indicated.

Let's apply what we've covered to the first two measures of a progression we looked at earlier, and at the same time introduce a very useful two-beat pattern called the **1 3 5 1 pattern**.

The 1 3 5 1 Pattern

The **1 3 5 1 pattern** outlines the triad and then returns to the root. All you need to do is change the solfege names to fit each chord. Here's the chord progression to the first two measures of "A Rhythm Thing" using the 1 3 5 1 pattern.

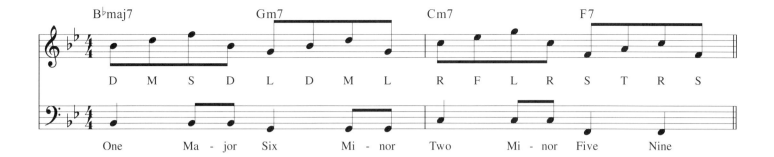

This pattern clearly and cleanly outlines the root movement and chord qualities for all four chords. But the pattern doesn't connect smoothly from the end of one chord to the beginning of the next chord, which makes it a little awkward to sing. Fortunately, there are other patterns that can help take care of that.

The 1 3 5 5 Pattern

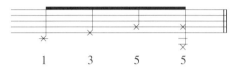

The **1 3 5 5 pattern** starts just like the previous pattern, but when you get to the last note, you can either repeat the previous pitch or drop it an octave. This second choice can be very useful when we want to keep the chord progression within a comfortable range for singing. It will also become useful when we need to take a breath, but more about that later. Here are the same two measures we looked at before, but now we're using the 1 3 5 5 pattern. Give yourself a starting DO and sing through it.

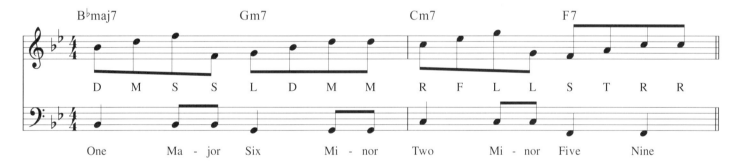

Now the connections between the chords are smoother. In the first measure, the octave drop is used between the I chord and the vi chord, but it's not used between the vi chord and the ii chord because it's not needed—the fifth of the vi chord is right next to the root of the ii chord. In the second measure, the octave drop is used to avoid severe range problems. These two patterns, 1 3 5 1 and 1 3 5 5, are very powerful, but there is still one more pattern to look at, the **1 3 5 3 pattern**.

The 1 3 5 3 Pattern

This pattern is especially useful when progressions move up by seconds or thirds. Since that doesn't happen with "A Rhythm Thing," we'll construct a short ascending chord progression to illustrate how to use it. Give yourself a starting DO and sing through the root movement of these two measures, then sing the chord outlines.

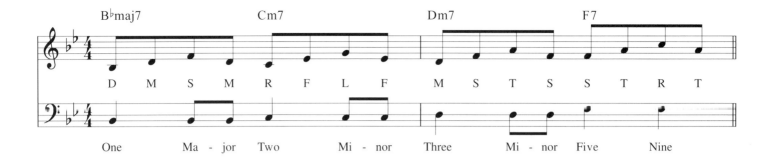

The 1 3 5 3 pattern ends on the third of each chord, a note that in this case is close to the root of the next chord making the connection smooth and easy.

Combining Patterns

All three patterns have their uses, and those of us who do this sort of thing have our favorites. For example, the 1 3 5 1 pattern works very well when progressions descend, as at the beginning of the following example. But we change to the 1 3 5 3 pattern when the progression ascends. Sing through this example.

Taking a Breath

One of the things you probably noticed as you sang through the previous example was that you almost ran out of breath before you got to the end of the fourth measure. As long as we're only limited to two or three measures, taking a breath really isn't necessary. But when progressions last four or more measures, breathing can become a problem. The solution is actually quite simple: just leave something out every few measures and take a breath. But the next question is "Where's a good place to take a breath?"

The solution is to leave out the fourth note of any pattern you're singing, as long as you can hear the root of the next chord easily. Let's look at the chord progression for the previous example and see what this means. We'll start by outlining all the notes as before. Then, we'll go back and circle the notes we plan to leave out, and circle the solfege as well. The result will look something like the next example.

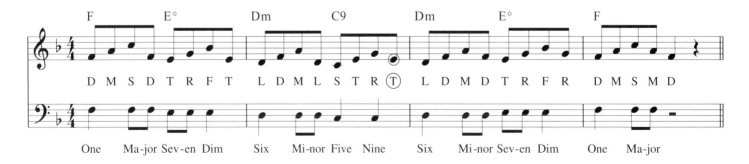

Going from RE (the fifth of the V chord) to LA (the root of the vi chord) is not hard to hear, so we now have a comfortable place to take a breath. That's all there is to it actually—just find a place you want to breathe, circle the notes and solfege, and go on with the progression. Once this becomes second nature, you'll be able to sing entire thirty-two-measure progressions without becoming winded.

Hearing and Outlining Sus Chords

Sus chords belong primarily to a special family of chords commonly found in jazz written during and after the '60s in which the third was replaced by a fourth. The chord symbols tell us whether the implied third is major or minor, but we don't exactly know how the sus chord functions—we only know how it sounds.

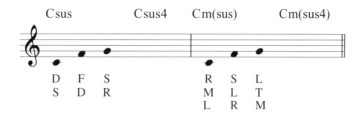

There are only two kinds of sus chords commonly used in jazz: one starts from SO and the other from RE. And if the chord symbol isn't written into an arrangement, it's hard to know which is which. Jazz theorist Jerry Coker believes that the only true sus chord is the V9(sus). So when in doubt, default to SO as the root of the chord. Ultimately, it won't make any difference in the sound of the chord. In fact, some jazz soloists have gotten around the issue completely by improvising solos that avoid the third of the chord altogether.

The following chord progression consists completely of sus chords. We will take Mr. Coker's lead and call them all "SO chords." For further study of sus chords, the author recommends looking at one of Herbie Hancock's most well-known compositions, "Maiden Voyage."

The Sus-chord Progression

TRACK 20

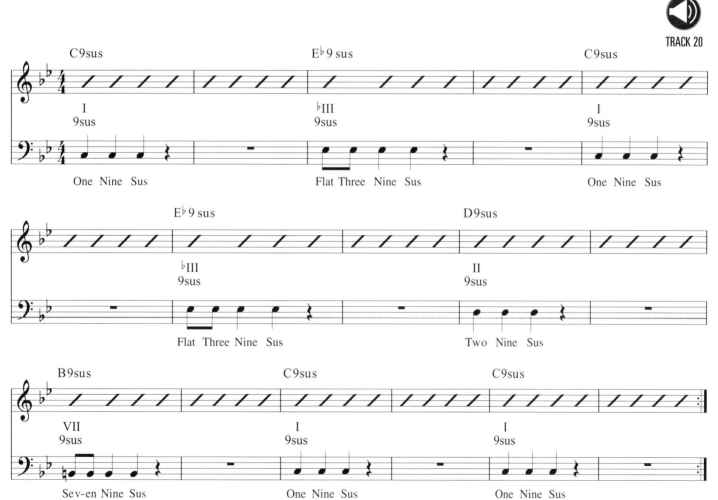

Hearing and Outlining Secondary Dominants

We pointed out earlier that secondary dominants are created in two ways: 1) by altering a diatonic chord; or 2) by borrowing a V chord from another key. They are always "SO chords" because they act as V chords of something, even though it may not be the I chord. Give yourself a starting note and sing through the root movement in the following example. Then sing through again, outlining the chords. Take a breath at the end of the second measure where the notes and solfege names are circled.

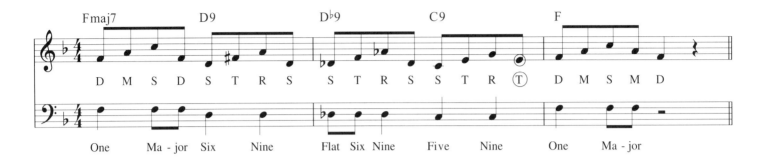

Notice how the three dominant chords move down chromatically. That's a sure sign that we're using a mix of chromatic and diatonic root movements for the secondary dominants, which means the 1 3 5 1 pattern will be the most effective choice.

Chromatic Diminished Sevenths

All chromatic diminished seventh chords should be thought of as vii chords that start with TI in a key other than the home key.

The F#°7 is a vii chord of G (the ii chord in F), and G#°7 is a vii chord of A (the iii chord in F). As long as you think of the diminished chord as a vii chord, you shouldn't have any problems labeling it and outlining it. Just remember that, because this is not an actual modulation, we don't call the chord following the diminished chord DO, but rather refer to it by its solfege and Roman numeral within the home key.

Augmented Chords

Earlier, when we explained diatonic triads, we went through major, minor, and diminished triads, but we left out the augmented triad. That was because augmented triads aren't diatonic to the major scale. When you raise the fifth note of a major triad, it becomes augmented, a triad that consists of two major thirds. The symbols used to indicate it are "aug," "(#5)," or "+." In this text we'll use the plus sign, "+." Augmented triads can be built from the I chord, the IV chord, or the V chord by raising the fifth. See the following example.

Augmented chords may sound strange to our ears at first, so here's a block drill to get the sound of the augmented triad linked up with the proper chromatic solfege names.

Block Drill: Learning to Hear the Augmented V chord

1. Give yourself a starting note.

2. Sing the following patterns several times, using the starting note to begin each pattern.

D – M – S – S̸ – S – M – D	D – M – S̸ – M – D
F – L – D – Ø – D – L – F	F – L – Ø – L – F
S – T – R – Ɍ – R – T – S	S – T – Ɍ – T – S

3. Give yourself a new starting note and repeat step 2.

When you can hear the augmented chord easily, you've completed this drill.

Here's how the above drill would look using a G augmented chord.

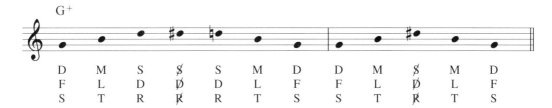

Of these three, the most commonly used augmented chord is the V9+ chord. It occurs far more often than either of the other two. The next in frequency is the Imaj7(♯5), which will occur when a I chord goes to a IV chord. The next example features a short progression that utilizes the augmented I chord and the augmented V chord. In addition, it's in 3/4. The CD track includes a demo of the example beginning with the root movement followed by the chord outlines. Listen to it, sing along, and then eliminate the voice track and sing it by yourself.

The Augmented Waltz

TRACK 21

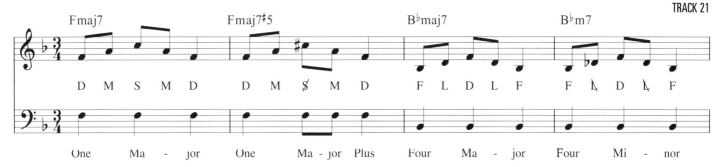

If the root movement gets too low for you, shift up an octave. You could shift up to B♭ in the third measure instead of down and then shift down from G to C at measures 7–8. Also notice that because the last note in each measure is a quarter note, we don't need to circle any notes in order to take a breath.

Chords Lasting for One Beat in 3/4 and 4/4

Chords can last for a whole measure in 3/4 meter, but sometimes two chords will occur in one measure. When that happens, the first chord almost always gets two beats and the second chord only one beat. Since we only have one beat, we use the root and third of the chord for outlining because they provide us with the most information; the root tells us the function and the third tells us the quality. So if, for example, we have a 3/4 measure with a ii chord lasting two beats followed by a V chord lasting one beat, the solution will look something like the next example in F.

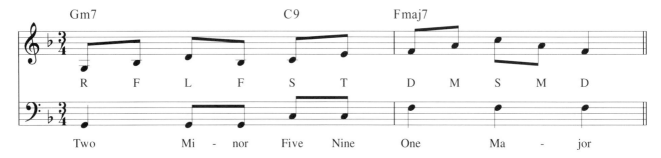

If we're working in 4/4, the solution is very similar. Here's one way to deal with a ii–V where each chord lasts only one beat.

This completes our introduction to ascending three-note chord patterns. Next we will add descending patterns to our arsenal for singing chord progressions.

Descending Three-Note Patterns

All descending three-note patterns begin from the root of the chord and move down to the fifth and then to the third: 8 5 3. There are three practical descending patterns: 8 5 3 1, 8 5 3 8, and 8 5 3 5.

The 8 5 3 1 Pattern

The 8 5 3 1 pattern can be very useful when a chord progression is starting to get to high to sing comfortably because it allows you to descend an octave.

The 8 5 3 8 Pattern

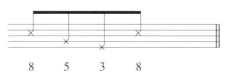

The 8 5 3 8 pattern is useful with chord progressions where the root movement moves down by half steps or whole steps. It is also very practical when roots move by fourths or fifths.

The 8 5 3 5 Pattern

Combining Ascending and Descending Patterns

The following is a sample progression that demonstrates how to combine ascending and descending patterns to add variety as you sing through chord progressions. The descending patterns are 8 5 3 5 and 8 5 3 1.

Next, we have another short progression that shows how to use the 8 5 3 8 pattern.

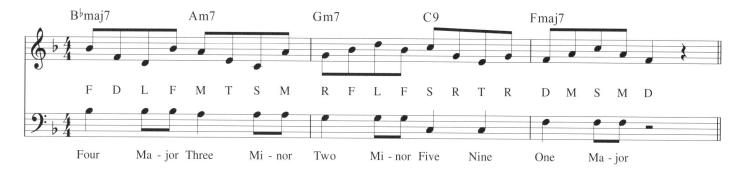

Hearing and Outlining Descending Sus Chords, Secondary Dominants, Chromatic vii° Chords, and Augmented Chords

All of these chords work the same way as their diatonic counterparts. The following includes two examples of how they might be found in actual progressions. The first progression has a descending E9sus using 8 5 4 1, a descending D9sus using 8 5 4 5, and a descending secondary dominant using 8 5 3 5.

The second progression has a descending V9+ using 8 5 3 5 and a chromatic vii° chord using 8 5 3 8.

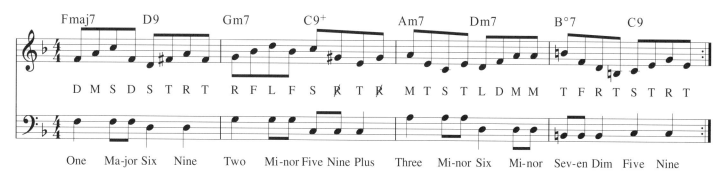

The following exercises give you a chance to internalize all the solfege names for the ascending and descending root position three-note chords presented so far. The exercises are written in the key of C, although they could be in any key.

Give yourself a starting note and sing through the exercises. Next, practice by giving yourself different starting notes and repeat the exercises several more times. Shift octaves whenever needed.

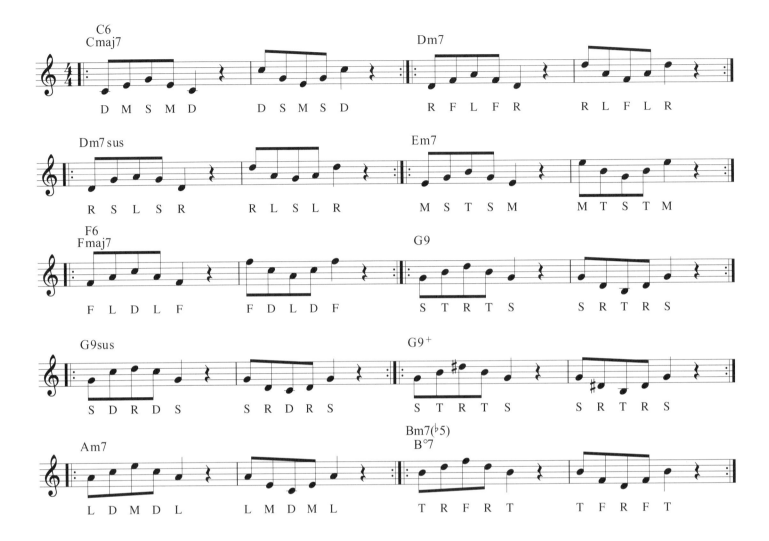

Chords Lasting for More than Two Beats

The following exercises present the common patterns for ascending and descending root position four-note chords. They are written in the key of C, although they could be in any key. Just as with the three-note patterns, give yourself a starting note and sing through the exercises, and then repeat the exercises using different starting notes.

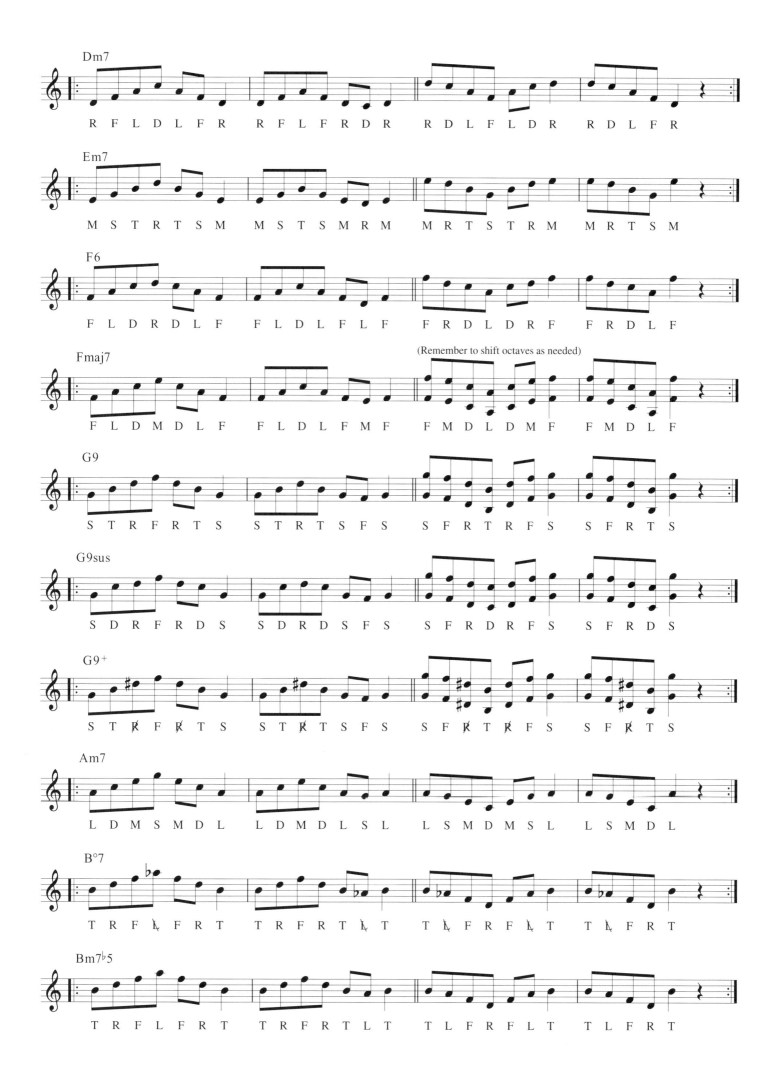

Once you've mastered these exercises, you're ready to move on to applying them to all kinds of chord progressions. So be sure and spend some time with them every day until they become second nature to you.

Finally, here are some examples that mix three- and four-note patterns together. Give yourself a starting DO, then sing through the root movements the first time and outline the chords the second time.

It is possible to handle a large number of chord progressions with what you know if you use a little intelligent guess work about the chords that haven't been covered yet.

6 Hearing and Outlining Inversions in Major

Inversions are used primarily to show how bass notes move in chord progressions. They tell us which note, other than the root, will be the lowest note in a chord. They don't affect the quality of the chord, only the way it is voiced—how the notes are laid out, from bottom to top.

Three-note Chord Inversions

The following example shows a chord progression using inversions. To indicate an inverted chord, a slash is placed after the chord name followed by the name of the note that will become the bass note. In our "root movement" line, a number is used instead of the name of the note, to tell us if the third, fifth, or some other note is in the bass, and to avoid confusing a chord function with a bass note. This is similar to what is done in classical music theory, where inversions are referred to by numbers (called "figured bass"). When singing an inversion such as the Gm7/B♭ in the second measure of the following example, use "Two Minor Bass 3" to indicate that the third is in the bass: the slash (/) means to sing the word "bass." Sing through the exercise beginning with the root movement, then outline the chords.

Listen to the track, noting where inversions occur and also where breaths have been suggested. When you are ready, sing along with the voice track—or remove it and sing the progression by yourself.

Exercise 1

TRACK 22

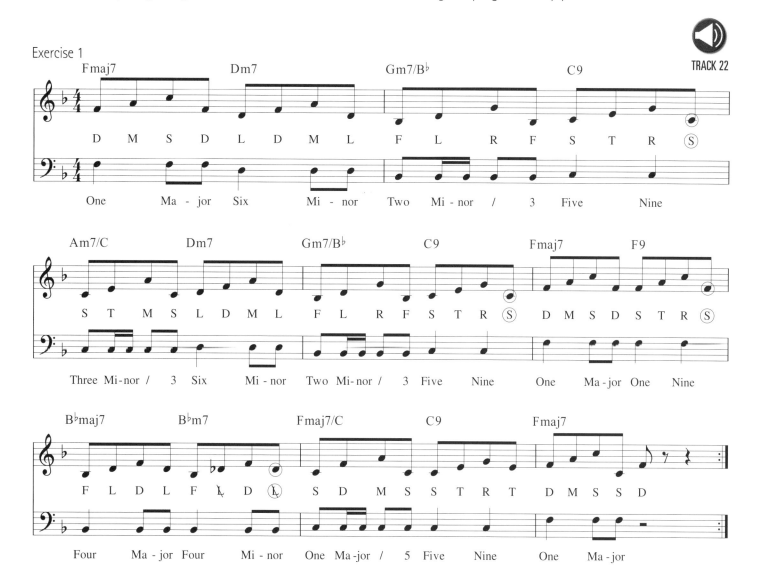

Don't be surprised if you had to pause and think about outlining these new chords. After all, this is new material and demands new skills and awareness.

The following exercises are intended to help you internalize the sound of three-note inversions. In the first exercise, the chords have the third as the lowest note. Give yourself a starting DO and sing through the exercise, then give yourself a new starting note and sing through the exercise again.

The chords in the next exercises have the fifth as the lowest note. Give yourself a starting note and sing through the exercise repeating any measure with multiple solfege names, then give yourself a new starting note and sing through the exercise again.

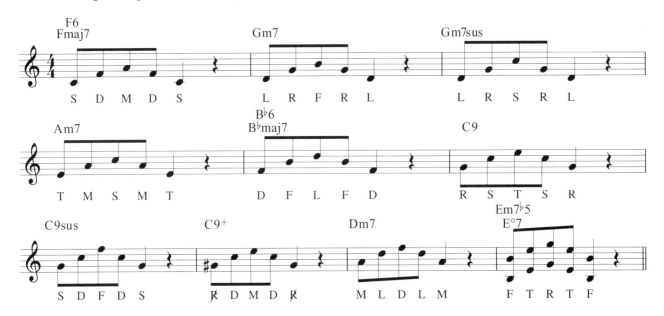

Here are some short exercises to allow you to practice working with inversions of three-note chords. Write in the correct solfege names under the treble-clef notes, then sing through the root movements and outline the chords. On the CD, the voice sings the root movements the first time through each example. Sing along with the voice track the first time through the exercise and then sing the chord outlines the second time through.

TRACK 23
Exercises 2–4

Exercise 2 in F

Exercise 3 in E♭

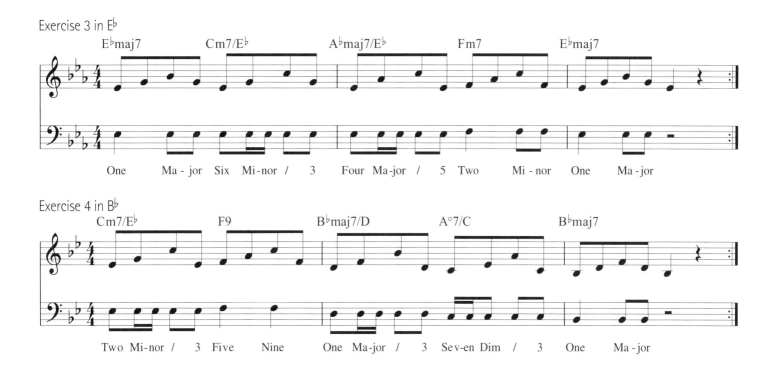

Exercise 4 in B♭

In addition to being a practical tool for outlining chord progressions, learning to hear and sing three-note inversions is an excellent introduction to handling four-note inversions. Mastery of this material will improve your ability to hear and recognize both three-note and four-note inversions.

Hearing and Outlining Four-Note Chord Inversions
First Inversions

Give yourself a starting note and sing through the following exercise, repeating any measures that give you difficulty.

Pay attention to the fully diminished chord in this exercise as you sing it and notice that even though it's inverted, the chord doesn't sound that way because all the notes are a minor third apart. Once you're feeling comfortable with this exercise, move on to chords with the fifth in the bass—second inversions.

Second Inversions

Give yourself a starting note and sing through the exercise, then give yourself a new starting note and sing through the exercise again.

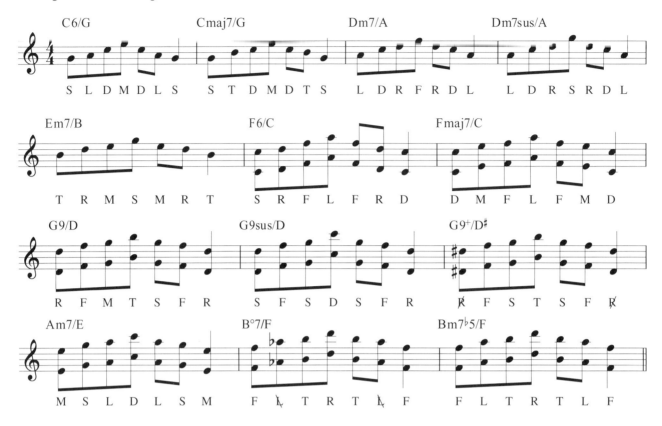

Again, notice that the diminished chord doesn't change in sound, even though the chord is written as an inversion. Most jazz musicians would probably write this chord as F°7 rather than B°7/F.

Third Inversions

The next exercise involves chords with the seventh in the bass—third inversions. This inversion will often follow a root position chord as, for example: Cmaj7 may be followed by Cmaj7/B, then followed by Am7. Or, Am7 may be followed by Am7/G, then Fmaj7.

Give yourself a starting note and sing through the exercise. Give yourself a new starting note and repeat the exercise.

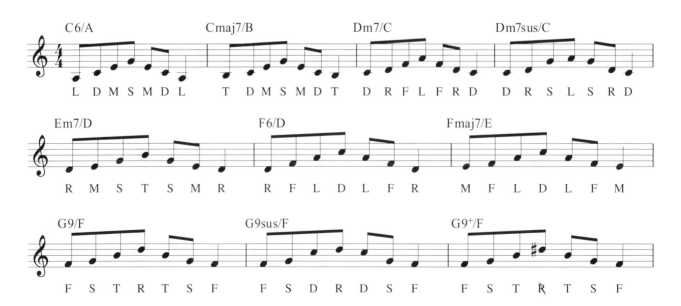

S L D M D L S T R F R T L T R F R T L

Next are some exercises for you to practice using inversions for four-note chords. Write in the solfege names for each exercise. As you will see, we've used a mix of three-note and four-note patterns for the root position chords, but focused on four-note patterns for inversions. In the first example, remember that the Cmaj7 chord begins with DO, but the C9/E chord doesn't because it is a secondary V chord.

On the CD, the piano plays the tonic of each key before the start of exercises 5, 6, and 7. Following the countoff, the voice sings the root movements the first time. Sing along with the voice track the first time through, then sing the chord outlines the second time.

TRACK 24
Exercises 5–7

Exercise 5 in C

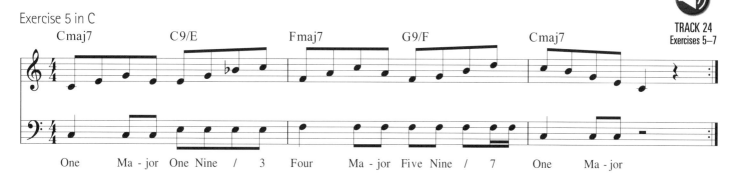

One   Ma - jor One Nine /   3   Four   Ma - jor Five Nine /   7   One   Ma - jor

The roots of this next example are completely diatonic, even though the V chord in measure 2 is augmented. This is why outlining the chord is so important: you'll never know that it's augmented by singing the root alone.

Exercise 6 in G

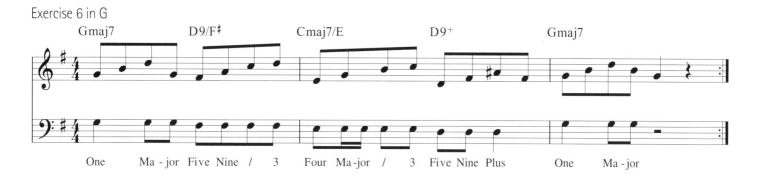

One   Ma - jor Five Nine /   3   Four Ma - jor /   3   Five Nine Plus   One   Ma - jor

Exercise 7 in B♭

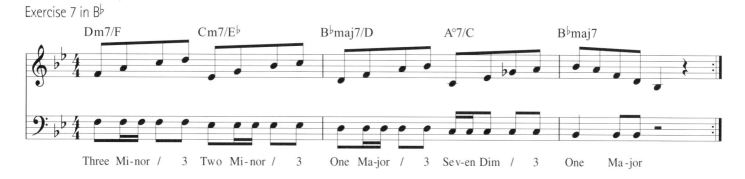

Three Mi - nor / 3 Two Mi - nor / 3   One Ma - jor / 3 Sev - en Dim / 3   One   Ma - jor

You will probably find these practice drills harder than most of what you will encounter in actual progressions, but having had to deal with them, you'll be able to figure out on your own what to do when a really complex chord progression turns up.

In addition to a study of sixteenth notes and jazz articulations, the second half of this book will examine how to apply what we have covered so far to music based on minor scales and minor chord progressions.

7 Hearing Chord-scales, Part One

"Chord-scales" is a term coined by jazz musicians to describe the relationship between a chord and the scales that contain the notes found in the chord. Chord-scales are the major scales, minor scales, and/or artificially created scales like the whole-tone scale or the diminished scale that can be used for soloing. There are often several possible chord-scales available for any chord. Those that are the most diatonic are referred to as being "inside" because their notes are all within the home key. Chord-scales borrowed from some other key are referred to as being "outside" because they contain one or more chromatic notes in relation to the home key. We will start by examining "inside" chord-scale choices.

Diatonic Chord-scales

Diatonic chord-scales are frequently referred to as **modes**. For example, the C major scale contains all the diatonic chords in the key of C. As a result, each mode is also the most "inside" chord-scale for the chord associated with it.

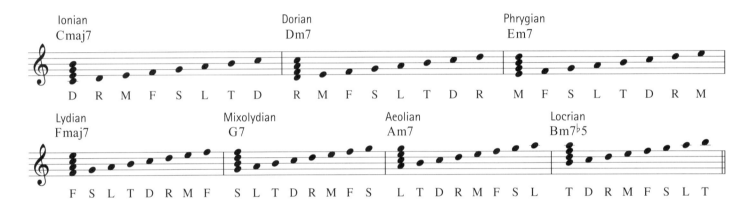

The following drills will help you internalize the sounds of the different modes of the major scale.

Block Drill: Ascending Modal Chord-scales in Major from a Common Note

Give yourself a starting note and call it DO. Sing up the major scale until you reach DO one octave higher, then stop and rest two beats. Go back to the original note you started with and call it RE. Starting from this same note, sing through the scale beginning with RE. When you reach RE one octave higher, stop and rest two beats. Go back to the original note you started from and call it MI. Starting from the same note, sing through the scale beginning with MI. When you reach MI one octave higher, stop and rest two beats. Each time you arrive at your starting note, one octave higher, rest two beats, skip down an octave and rename it to become the starting note of the next modal scale.

DRMFSLTD	RMFSLTDR	MFSLTDRM	FSLTDRMF
SLTDRMFS	LTDRMFSL	TDRMFSLT	DRMFSLTD

Here's an example of how the beginning of this drill would look starting from G.

The difference between half steps and whole steps will become apparent as you work on this material. Don't give up if it seems really demanding—it takes time to master this. Some students have taken weeks to become proficient at this drill. While you're working on it, go ahead and practice other things, but keep coming back here until you can do it. It will help you to start hearing new key centers quickly and begin to recognize when soloists are using modal chord-scales.

Note: There's an easy way to figure out a mode—such as G Phrygian, for example. First, you must know that Phrygian is the third mode, then ask yourself the question: "G is the third degree in what major scale?" E♭ major is the answer, so G Phrygian is an E♭ major scale starting on the third note, G.

Once you've finished this block drill, start on the next one. It will also be demanding because we often have more trouble recognizing and singing descending intervals than ascending intervals.

Block Drill: Descending Modal Chord-scales in Major from a Common Note

Give yourself a starting note and call it DO. Sing down the major scale until you reach DO one octave lower, then stop and rest two beats. Go back to the original note you started with and call it TI. Starting from this same note, sing through the scale beginning with TI. When you reach TI one octave lower, stop and rest two beats. Go back to the original note you started with and call it LA. Starting from this same original note, sing through the scale beginning with LA. When you reach LA one octave lower, stop and rest two beats. Each time you arrive at your starting note one octave lower, rest two beats, skip up an octave, and rename it to become the starting note of the next modal scale.

DTLSFMRD	TLSFMRDT	LSFMRDTL	SFMRDTLS
FMRDTLSF	MRDTLSFM	RDTLSFMR	DTLSFMRD

Here is how the beginning of the descending block drill would look starting from G.

The Lydian-tonic Scale

Modern jazz musicians have gravitated towards replacing the major scale with the **Lydian scale**, producing a slightly "outside" sound when soloing. The Lydian scale is normally associated with the IV chord, and is like a major scale with a raised fourth degree. However, when it's associated with a I chord, the solfege names change to reflect that this is a tonic sound, thus the **Lydian-tonic** name.

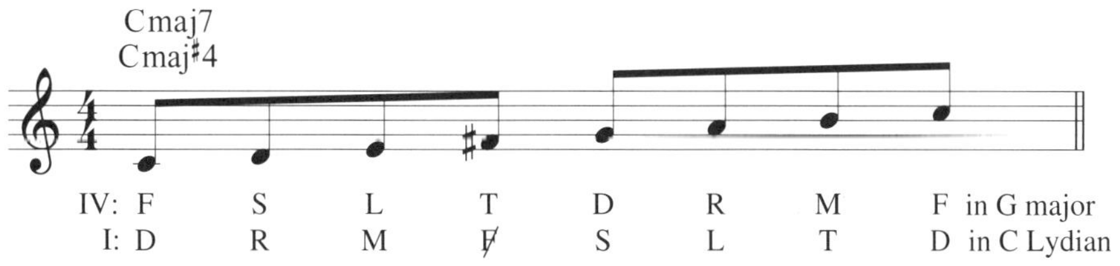

Use the following block drill to become familiar with the solfege names for both chord-scales.

Block Drill: Hearing the Lydian and Lydian-tonic Chord-scales

1. Give yourself a starting note and call it FA. Sing up the Lydian chord-scale until you reach FA an octave higher. Rest two beats. Change the name of the starting note to DO and sing up the Lydian-tonic chord-scale. Rest two beats.
2. Give yourself a new starting note and call it FA. Sing down the Lydian chord-scale and rest two beats. Change the name of the starting note to DO and sing down the Lydian-tonic chord-scale. Rest two beats.

Repeat steps 1 and 2 until you're comfortable with the solfege names for the Lydian-tonic chord-scale.

Remember: If the I chord consistently has a ♯4 or ♯11 added, then the progression is treating the I chord as a Lydian-tonic, and the chord-scale starts from DO.

The Blues-tonic Chord-scale

Anyone familiar with jazz knows that the blues is a significant part of the music jazz musicians perform. Over the years many blues chord progressions have been written that replace the I chord with a I9 chord. But the I9 chord is thought of as functioning as a normal I chord—in other words, a DO chord. This means the chord-scale for a I9 chord functioning as a I chord should start from DO also.

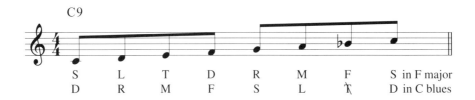

As you can see above, this scale is like the major scale with lowered seventh, which is sometimes called the Mixolydian scale. But when we treat this scale with the I9 chord as a tonic, we refer to this as a **blues-tonic**. Here's how the first four measures of a blues tune might work out using a blues-tonic for the I chord in C major.

Like the Lydian-tonic chord-scale, the blues-tonic chord-scale can easily be learned using a simple block drill.

Block Drill: Hearing the Mixolydian and Blues-tonic Chord-scales

1. Give yourself a starting note and call it SO. Sing up the Mixolydian chord-scale until you reach SO an octave higher. Rest two beats. Change the name of the starting note to DO and sing up the blues-tonic chord-scale (you'll be singing the same pitches, just different solfege names). Rest two beats.

2. Give yourself a new starting note and call it SO. Sing down the Mixolydian chord-scale, then rest two beats. Change the name of the starting note to DO and sing down the blues-tonic chord-scale. Rest two beats.

Repeat steps 1 and 2 until you're comfortable with the solfege names for the blues-tonic chord-scale.

The Bebop Chord-scale Family

An interesting thing happens when we descend through the chord-scales of the major scale, no matter which chord-scale we use: the chord tones don't line up with the scale notes on each downbeat. For example, if we descend in eighth notes using the G major scale, the first note is G, a chord tone, but from there on, the chord tones don't line up for the second, third, and fourth beats.

It didn't take jazz musicians very long to figure out that this wasn't a good thing. To fix the problem, they created a family of chord-scales based on the major, Mixolydian (dominant), and Dorian modes that allowed ascending and descending melodic ideas to have their chord tones line up with each downbeat. These chord-scales are referred to as the bebop major, bebop dominant, and bebop Dorian. They are sometimes called "passing-tone chord-scales" because they're created by adding a single passing tone to an otherwise diatonic mode. Let's look at the bebop major chord-scale first.

Bebop Major

The **bebop major** scale adds a minor sixth as a passing tone to the major scale.

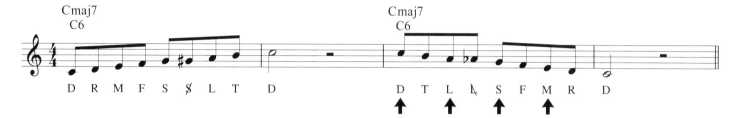

The bebop major scale works nicely for both ascending and descending scales. All the primary chord tones line up with chord-scales on the beats. SO becomes SI going up, and LA becomes LE going down.

Bebop Dominant

The **bebop dominant** scale adds a major seventh, FI, as a passing tone. It too works nicely for both ascending and descending melodic ideas. What is especially important is that with descending ideas, the passing note, SE, allows the minor seventh FA, to fall on a downbeat, along with all the other chord tones.

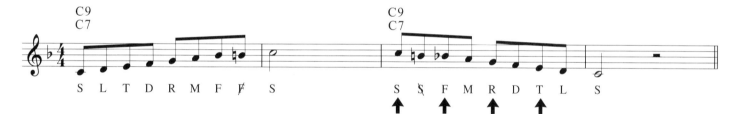

Bebop Dorian

The **bebop Dorian** chord-scale adds a major third as a passing tone. This chord-scale is, however, more specialized. If the chord lasts four beats, the first half of the scale lines up well, but the second half doesn't.

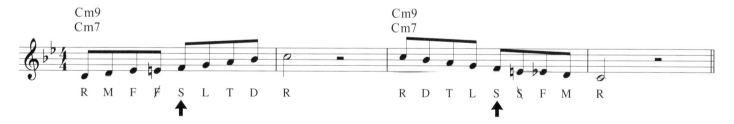

However, when a ii–V progression occurs within a single measure, the bebop Dorian scale is ideally suited for use. As a result, most soloists tend to limit their use of the bebop Dorian chord-scale to chord progressions where each chord of the ii–V formula lasts two beats.

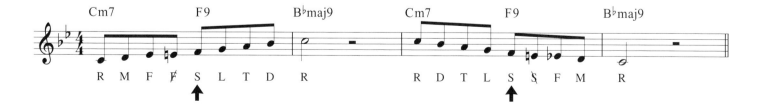

Here's a block drill to help you learn to hear these chord-scales.

> **Block Drill: The Bebop Family of Chord-scales**
>
> 1. Give yourself a starting RE and sing up and down the bebop Dorian scale in eighth notes.
> 2. Using the same reference note, change the name to SO and sing up and down the bebop dominant scale in eighth notes.
> 3. Using the same reference note, change the name to DO and sing up and down the bebop major scale in eighth notes.
> 4. Start with a new note and repeat steps 1 through 3 several times.
>
> When you can recall any bebop chord-scale easily, you've passed this drill.

This is how the drill would look beginning with C.

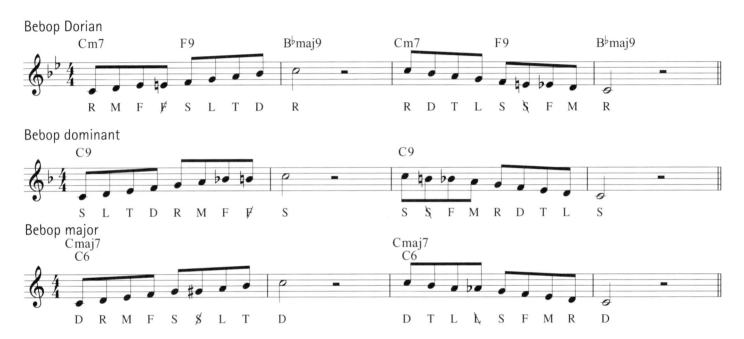

It doesn't matter if we are using modes or bebop scales. By getting the sounds of different chord-scales into our heads, we enrich our possibilities for soloing.

The Diminished Scale

The **diminished scale** (dim) is a chromatic chord-scale which has no DO present, only a raised DO. This scale, associated with diminished chords, begins with TI and alternates whole steps and half steps, producing a combination of chromatic and diatonic pitches. There are only three different diminished scales, each of which is one half step higher than the preceding one. And, depending on the key signature, the spelling of these scales will vary. But no matter how they are spelled, we keep the solfege names the same.

Look at the first diminished scale, D°7. It's the vii of E♭. All the notes and solfege names match, although most musicians will probably spell C♭ as B♮. In the second chord-scale, D♮ replaces C✕ which is LI in the key of E major; the reason is obvious—no one wants to deal with C✕ unless they absolutely have to. The third chord-scale matches up with the solfege names.

Now let's look at the descending diminished chord-scales. In the descending D°7 scale E♮ replaces F♭. Again, this is more for reading purposes than anything else. In the D♯°7 scale all the notes match up. In the E°7 scale, F♯ replaces G♭.

Notice that it doesn't matter if the scale is ascending or descending; we've made the first note of each beat a chord tone and the last beat has been made into a triplet in order to fit everything into four beats (notice that each scale has eight different pitches).

Here's a block drill to help you learn to hear the diminished scale and its resolution to DO.

Block Drill: Resolving Diminished Scales to DO

1. Give yourself a starting TI and sing up the scale in eighth notes using a triplet for the last beat. Resolve the last note up to DO.

2. Using DO as your reference, change the name to TI and sing down the scale in eighth notes using a triplet for the last beat. Resolve the last note up to DO.

3. Repeat steps 1 and 2 using a new DO.

Repeat the drill many times until you can easily hear and sing the ascending and descending diminished scale, and resolve it to DO.

This is how the first two exercises in the drill would look starting from D♯.

The Whole-tone Scale

The **whole-tone scale** (WTS), like the diminished scale, is artificially created. It has only six tones and, because all the notes are the same distance apart, any note can theoretically be the starting note. This is why it becomes useful to assign one of the notes to serve as the root of both the scale and the chord.

The principal application of this scale is with dominant chords that have ♯5 and ♯11 or ♭5 and ♭13, so the starting note is SO, not DO. The following examples show the ascending and descending forms of the whole-tone scale starting from G and A♭.

The same principles apply for the whole-tone scale and the diminished scale: both are spelled to make reading easier; as a result, the solfege names may not match the written notes. In the previous example, the notes and names both match. But that's not the case when they descend.

The descending G whole-tone scale changes C♯ to D♭ and D♯ to E♭ without any trouble. The descending A♭ whole-tone scale keeps E♮ instead of changing to F♭, and keeps the D♮ as well. Who wants to think of E♭♭? Nonetheless, the solfege names need to change, so RI changes to ME and DI changes to RA.

Like the diminished scale, the whole-tone scale needs to be resolved to a note that's not present in the scale.

Since there are only six notes in the scale, add an eighth note in 4/4 meter to complete the measure, then resolve the scale to DO in the next measure.

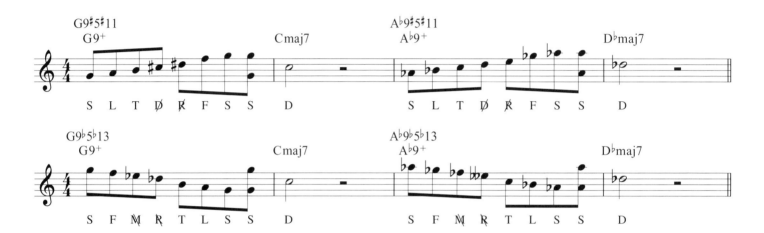

By adding an eighth note, you can shift up or down an octave to stay within your range.

Here's a block drill to help you hear the resolution of a whole-tone scale.

> **Block Drill: The Whole-tone Scale**
>
> 1. Give yourself a starting note and sing through the ascending pattern starting on SO, then resolve the scale to DO.
>
> 2. Change the name from DO to SO and sing the descending pattern down from that note, resolving to a new DO.
>
> Repeat this drill many times until you can sing it easily.

Remember: As with the diminished scale, conflicts often occur between the best way to notate the whole-tone scale visually and what the notes represent in solfege. When this happens, the respelled (enharmonic) notes are there to improve sight reading only, and the solfege names don't change.

This scale was well-liked by tenor saxophonist Lester Young, who loved to use it to replace the chord-scales normally used with unaltered V chords. In other words, Young used it as an "outside" scale. Lester knew that certain notes clashed with the diatonic notes of the unaltered chords, but he liked the whole-tone scale—and that was that!

Dictation Exercise: Hearing Chord-scales

The different chord-scales presented in this chapter are covered in this dictation exercise. There are
is heard either ascending or
ur choice by writing it in the blank
sponses with the answers that are
vs: major, Dorian, Phrygian, Lydian,
it, whole-tone, and diminished. If
sheet of paper.

_____ 4) _____

_____ 8) _____

_____ 12) _____

_____ 16) _____

_____ 20) _____

_____

in enrich your possibilities for soloing.
articular chord-scale, you shouldn't

ns

s for soloing. In order to practice hear-
gressions. To do so, follow these steps.

:o test out some chord-scales.

measure exercise.

to use when you solo.

i–V–I progression. Earlier in this chap-
r these chords are Dorian, Mixolydian,
in the key of F major. There are

optional pauses to take a breath at the end of each measure.

Exercise 1

Gm7   C9   Fmaj7

R M F S L T D R S F M R D T L S D R M F S L T D

ANSWERS, Track 25: 1) Mixolydian; 2) Phrygian; 3) Whole-tone; 4) Major; 5) Dorian; 6) Lydian; 7) Bebop dominant; 8) Dorian; 9) Diminished; 10) Locrian; 11) Major; 12) Whole-tone; 13) Phrygian; 14) Bebop minor; 15) Aeolian; 16) Mixolydian; 17) Lydian; 18) Diminished; 19) Locrian; 20) Bebop major; 21) Bebop minor; 22) Aeolian; 23) Bebop major.

Now here's the same example, but we've adjusted the last notes of the Gm7 and C9 chord-scales in order to help them connect to the starting notes of the following chord-scales more smoothly. Other than that, they're still just ascending and descending scales.

Exercise 2

Sing through both examples and take your pick of how you want to do this. Either way, these examples will help you to hear the "inside" chord-scales for these chords.

If we want to apply this principle to chords that change every two beats, all we do is switch from eighth notes to sixteenth notes. Our ii–V–I progression now looks like the next example, and it will sound almost identical to the previous exercise, but faster. And because it is faster, we probably won't need to take a breath until the exercise is finished.

Exercise 3

What we've done using the ii–V–I progression is model how to practice applying and hearing chord-scales.

Chromatic Chord-scales

In the following exercise, chromatic movement of the bass encourages us to complete the chord-scales for the Gm7 and Gb9 chords, rather than use the adjusted version we used in Exercise 3. Also, you will see that we've included a Lydian-tonic chord-scale for the I chord. Sing through this exercise.

Exercise 4

Exercise 5 uses three chromatic V chords in a row. The first two are examples of complete chord-scales because the roots move chromatically. The last two have been adjusted to allow for smoother connections.

Exercise 5

This chapter should give you a good introduction to chord-scales. Feel free to start applying this material to your tune-learning to expand your soloing vocabulary. We'll be taking this idea up again later in the second part of this book when we study minor chord progressions.

Dictation Exercise: Hearing Chord-scales

TRACK 25

The different chord-scales presented in this chapter are covered in this dictation exercise. There are twenty-three scales played on Track 25, all of which start from C; each is heard either ascending or descending. After each scale is played, stop the recording and make your choice by writing it in the blank provided. When you are finished with the entire CD track, check your responses with the answers that are listed upside-down at the bottom of the page. The choices are as follows: major, Dorian, Phrygian, Lydian, Mixolydian, Aeolian, Locrian, bebop major, bebop minor, bebop dominant, whole-tone, and diminished. If you wish to do this exercise again, write your responses on a separate sheet of paper.

1) _____ 2) _____ 3) _____ 4) _____

5) _____ 6) _____ 7) _____ 8) _____

9) _____ 10) _____ 11) _____ 12) _____

13) _____ 14) _____ 15) _____ 16) _____

17) _____ 18) _____ 19) _____ 20) _____

21) _____ 22) _____ 23) _____

By getting the sounds of different chord-scales into your head, you can enrich your possibilities for soloing. It's also important to remember that if you can't hear the notes in a particular chord-scale, you shouldn't use them when it comes time to solo.

Applying Chord-scales to Progressions

Next, we have a practical way to go about learning to hear chord-scales for soloing. In order to practice hearing chord-scales effectively, we need to apply them to actual chord progressions. To do so, follow these steps.

Step 1

Locate a short section of a chord progression where you want to test out some chord-scales.

Step 2

Isolate the section and then turn it into a one-, two-, or three-measure exercise.

Step 3

Sing through the progression using the chord-scales you want to use when you solo.

Let's try this out using the most common chord formula in jazz, the ii–V–I progression. Earlier in this chapter we pointed out that the diatonic ("inside") chord-scale choices for these chords are Dorian, Mixolydian, and major. The following example shows what these would look like in the key of F major. There are optional pauses to take a breath at the end of each measure.

TRACK 26
Exercises 1–5

Exercise 1

Now here's the same example, but we've adjusted the last notes of the Gm7 and C9 chord-scales in order to help them connect to the starting notes of the following chord-scales more smoothly. Other than that, they're still just ascending and descending scales.

Exercise 2

R M F S L T D L S F M R D T L T D R M F S L T D

Sing through both examples and take your pick of how you want to do this. Either way, these examples will help you to hear the "inside" chord-scales for these chords.

If we want to apply this principle to chords that change every two beats, all we do is switch from eighth notes to sixteenth notes. Our ii–V–I progression now looks like the next example, and it will sound almost identical to the previous exercise, but faster. And because it is faster, we probably won't need to take a breath until the exercise is finished.

Exercise 3

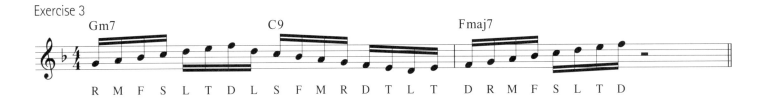

R M F S L T D L S F M R D T L T D R M F S L T D

What we've done using the ii–V–I progression is model how to practice applying and hearing chord-scales.

Chromatic Chord-scales

In the following exercise, chromatic movement of the bass encourages us to complete the chord-scales for the Gm7 and G♭9 chords, rather than use the adjusted version we used in Exercise 3. Also, you will see that we've included a Lydian-tonic chord-scale for the I chord. Sing through this exercise.

Exercise 4

R M F S L T D R S F M R D T L S D R M F♯ S L T D D

Exercise 5 uses three chromatic V chords in a row. The first two are examples of complete chord-scales because the roots move chromatically. The last two have been adjusted to allow for smoother connections.

Exercise 5

S L T D R M F S S F M R D T L S S L T D R M F R S F M R D T L T D

This chapter should give you a good introduction to chord-scales. Feel free to start applying this material to your tune-learning to expand your soloing vocabulary. We'll be taking this idea up again later in the second part of this book when we study minor chord progressions.

Section Two

8 Hearing Jazz Rhythms and Articulations, Part Two

Alternating Straight Sixteenths with Swing Eighths

As the value of the notes subdivides beyond eighth-note triplets, a point is reached where there is no longer any significant difference between swing feel and the straight-eighth feel of simple notation. In fact, often when performing a piece with swing feel, sixteenth notes will be played straight, even though the surrounding eighth notes are swung.

Classical musicians are taught to count sixteenth notes using "one-ee-and-uh, two-ee-and-uh," and so on. There's even a shorthand for writing sixteenth notes: "1 e + a, 2 e + a." This system certainly works for locating where notes start, but tells us nothing about durations or articulations, two important elements in performing jazz correctly. Of course, the traditional system for counting was never intended to be used for singing melodies, only for chanting rhythms on one note. The syllables for counting or singing sixteenth notes in jazz are "Doo-Be-dah-buh," and the shorthand is (D B d b, D B d b). As with eighth notes, the first and second syllables are capitalized to show that they occur during the first half of the beat. The third and fourth syllables are not capitalized.

Unlike jazz eighth-note syllables, sixteenth-note syllables don't need to be treated differently when they're followed by rests—it just depends on how long a note lasts.

In the above example, beats 1 and 2 use the same syllables as beats 3 and 4, but the downbeat of beat 1 is an eighth note, so it's longer than the downbeat sixteenth note of beat 3. Use a long "Dooo" for beat 1 and a short "Do" for beat 3. Now look at the next measure.

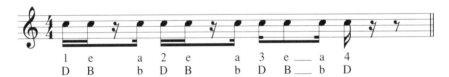

This time the second note in beat 3 is an eighth note, so it's held out. Think of it as two sixteenths tied together. To perform this accurately, use "Doo Be buh" for beats 1 and 2, and "Do Beee buh" for beat 3.

Exercise 1 is an example of a section of straight sixteenth notes in the middle of a tune written with a swing feel. Good jazz performers will really lay into the eighth notes to emphasize the change to the swing feel in the second half of measure 3. Listen a few times, then eliminate the voice track. Give yourself your own starting note and sing the exercise.

Exercise 1

TRACK 27

In Exercise 2, the entire section remains in a straight sixteenth-note feel (no swing on the eighth notes). Music written like this might occur as part of a harmonized ensemble passage in a jazz ballad, for example. Listen to and practice this exercise as before.

Exercise 2

TRACK 28

Staccato Notes at the Sixteenth-note Level

In Chapter 1 when we talked about eighth notes, the syllable "dit" was used to indicate how staccato notes were to be performed. When jazz moves to the sixteenth-note level, staccato sixteenth notes take on a similar function, so we also call them "dit." Staccato eighths and sixteenths are the shortest notes we normally encounter in jazz. In addition, there is almost no difference between a staccato eighth note performed at a moderate swing tempo and a staccato sixteenth note performed at, for example, a typical funk tempo (which is usually about half the speed of a swing tempo). Since all staccato notes are expected to sound the same, it makes no sense to use different syllables, so think "dit" for both staccato eighths and sixteenths whenever they're called for. Exercise 3 demonstrates normal and staccato upbeat sixteenth notes.

Exercise 3

TRACK 29

Find some examples of fusion, jazz/rock, and funk tunes and apply the rhythmic syllables covered here to help you in learning the melodies and accompaniment parts. Bass parts are particularly challenging to work on.

Specialized Jazz Notation

There are numerous specialized melodic and rhythmic devices that have given jazz its unique flavor. Some are primarily centered in performance practices of big-band ensemble music. Others, such as ghosted notes and glissandi, continue to remain quite popular in all styles of jazz. All are normally associated with swing feel because that's where they originated.

The Sixteenth-Note Triplet

Sixteenth–note triplets occur frequently as melodic ornaments in music with a swing feel. The interesting thing about this type of triplet is that it occurs rhythmically within another triplet. Since the eighth notes of jazz music are uneven, the so-called sixteenth-note triplet takes place during the first two-thirds of the beat, which means it really isn't made from sixteenth notes. Unfortunately, we don't have a standard notation to indicate accurately what the true value of the triplet notes should be. "Doo-ee-uh" is recommended for performing the sixteenth-note triplet itself. When combined with the upbeat jazz eighth note ("duh"), the two together produce "Doo-ee-uh-duh." Listen to Track 30 a few times; then eliminate the voice track, giving yourself your own starting note to sing the exercise.

TRACK 30

Exercise 4

Reminder: To perform the sixteenth-note triplet correctly, the triplet needs to be spread out evenly across the first two-thirds of the beat, not crowded into the very beginning of the beat.

The Jazz Turn

The **jazz turn** is quite the opposite of the sixteenth-note triplet in execution. It occurs on the last half of the beat (which is technically the last third of the beat) as a triplet. It is usually found with notes lasting at least one beat and often longer, and is performed at the end of the note, just before the start of the next note. As with triplet sixteenth notes, the syllables that represent the jazz turn are "Doo-ee-uh," but with the entire triplet coming as late as is needed. Listen to Track 31 a few times, then eliminate the voice track. Sing Exercise 5 by giving yourself your own starting note.

TRACK 31

Exercise 5

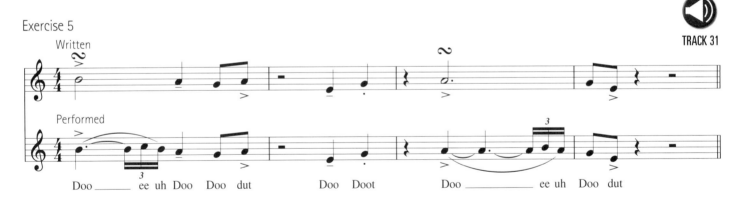

Ghosted Notes

A note is **ghosted** when it is played dramatically softer than the notes on either side of it. Other terms for ghosted notes are "swallowed notes" and "indefinite sounds." The syllable that closely duplicates ghosting is created by using a swallowed "n" sound. Because ghosted notes are primarily an upbeat phenomenon, it's useful to add a "d" to the word "Doo" to produce "Dood-n" when trying to imitate this fairly common jazz articulation. "Dood-n" represents a normal downbeat note followed by a ghosted upbeat; "dud-n" represents a normal upbeat note followed by a ghosted upbeat.

Ghosted notes are indicated in the music by placing parentheses around the notehead or by replacing the notehead itself with an "x," as in Exercise 6. This effect is most commonly reserved for lower notes found within a phrase and generally affects upbeats, although passages using triplets can have ghosted notes as well.

When practicing Example 6, listen to Track 32 a few times, then eliminate the voice track. Give yourself your own starting note when you're ready to sing the exercise.

Exercise 6

Dood -n Dood -n Doo dut   Doo   Doo duh Dood - n Dood - n   Doo duh ___   Dood -n Doo dut

Grace Notes

The **single jazz grace note** is generally performed on the beat (downbeat or upbeat) of the main note, rather than before the primary note. The syllable "D'oo" captures the illusion of two notes (the grace note and primary note) sounded together for downbeats, and "D'uh" portrays the illusion of swing upbeats.

D'oo   D'oo   Dit   duh   Doo   dut   D'uh   Dood - n   Doo   dut

Double jazz grace notes will be sung with the syllables "dah-buh," taken from the last half of a sixteenth-note pattern. Example 7 adds two more measures to the end of the previous example, including double jazz grace notes. Practice singing Exercise 7 after listening to Track 33. For a challenge, try singing the exercise before you listen to the CD track, then listen and try again. As you've done before, choose your own starting pitch.

Exercise 7

D'oo   D'oo   Dit duh Doo dut   D'uh   Dood - n Doo dut   dah buh Doo duh Doo dut

Most of the following articulations are associated with big band music. As such, they are valuable for instrumentalists and conductors alike who may not be familiar with how these symbols should sound in performance.

The Fall or Downward Gliss

The **fall**, also known as the **downward gliss**, involves dropping or falling downward from the main note at the end of its duration. The beginning note of a fall will usually be given an accent, and the fall itself will be either short, full, or long, depending on what is desired for effect. The length of the fall is usually indicated by the length of the fall sign itself, although the words "long" or "long fall" may be added to indicate very long effects. Sometimes a minus sign and a number will be added to indicate exactly where the fall is to end. The symbol "-3" means the fall should end on beat three of the next measure. There is no specific ending pitch for a fall because the note is intended to die away to nothing as it ends.

The syllable "Dow" captures the sound of the fall and the gliss. In performing "Dow," the voice should drop in pitch after the initial attack and then die away. Remember to practice using short, full, and long falls in order to capture the proper effect.

Exercise 8

Doo _____   dow ____   Dat   Doo _____   dow _____

Though the terms "fall" and "gliss" are often used interchangeably, there is a difference. The gliss is more of a rapid diatonic or chromatic drop, with a clearer definition of individual pitches instead of a slide. Saxophone players perform the gliss in place of the fall because the fall isn't comfortable for reed players to execute. The notation for the saxophone gliss is a wavy line attached to the note.

The Connecting Gliss

The **connecting gliss** involves joining two notes by filling-in the space between them. A connecting gliss can occur from low to high or high to low. In either case, the second note will receive a slight accent. The syllable for the first note of the connecting gliss will be "Doo" or "duh," depending on whether the note is an upbeat or a downbeat. The beginning of the second word will change from "Yoo" to "yuh" depending on if the connecting gliss ends with a downbeat or upbeat. Brass parts usually use a straight line (top line below) and reed parts use a wavy line (bottom). The results are the same.

Exercise 9

TRACK 35

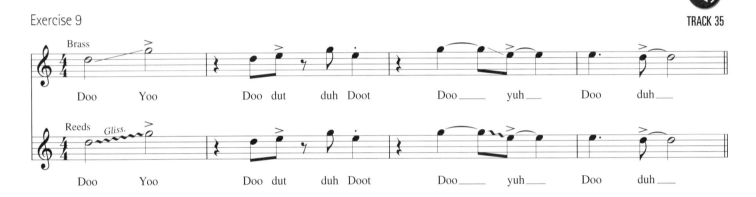

The Upward Gliss

The **upward gliss**, sometimes called a "squeeze," occurs before the beginning of a note and can be approximated using the syllables "Yoo" or "yuh." The "Y" sound actually starts the note.

Exercise 10

TRACK 36

The Shake

Shakes are used primarily in big band arrangements to add drama to the music. Shakes move back and forth rapidly between two notes, similar to the trill found in classical music. But the shake differs in that it is usually slower, and the distance between the two notes is wider.

If the shake begins with a downbeat, the syllables "Doo-ee-oo-ee-oot" (continuing the vowels as long as is needed) can be used, while for upbeats, the syllables are "duh-ee-ah-ee-aht." Shakes are often performed as triplets or sixteenth notes depending on the tempo of the piece. It is best to have the shake end on the last downbeat before going to the next note or rest. Exercise 11 combines the shake and the fall.

Exercise 11

TRACK 37

Doo - ee - oo - ee - oo - oot Dow_____   Dat   dah - ee - ah - ee - aht dow

Mastering shakes, whether on your instrument or sung, takes time. Being able to reproduce them means you are aware of them and understand what they might sound like when you encounter them in written music.

The Flip

The **flip** is followed by a downbeat staccato note. It involves three notes, two of which are indicated and one which is implied. The syllables for performing the flip are "Doo-ee-oot." The flip takes place as the last third of an eighth-note triplet, but the note performed may be as much as a perfect fourth above the written note, as in Exercise 12. Although the "flipped" note doesn't have to be a perfect fourth, it's usually at least a third above the written note. Listen to Track 38 to get a better idea of how this sounds. The example helps by showing you how this actually sounds as well as how it is written.

Exercise 12

TRACK 38

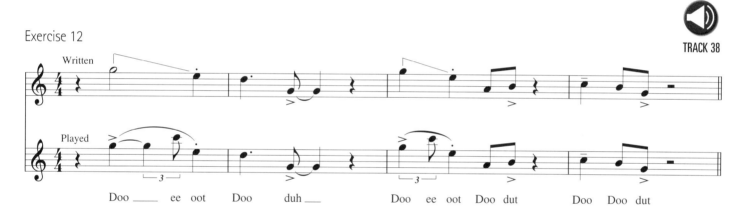

Doo____ ee oot Doo duh____   Doo ee oot Doo dut   Doo Doo dut

The Doit

The **doit** (rhymes with "boy," followed by a "t") involves bending upward from the end of the principal note at the end of the beat. Although there is a definite beginning to the doit, there is no definite ending pitch because the sound is intended to die away as the note ends. In vocalizing the doit, the voice should dramatically rise in pitch as the "oit" portion of the syllable progresses. The symbol is similar to a slur, bending upward, ending "unattached."

Exercise 13

TRACK 39

Doit   Dat Doit   Dat Doo Doo duh Doo dut   Doit

When doits are played in some professional bands, a contest among the brass often occurs to see who will end the doit last. The results can be quite comical, to say the least. Obviously, to avoid this it may be useful to mark the ending point clearly.

The Du-wah

"Du" and "Wah" are names for a brass technique in which the hand is placed over the opening of the bell (Du) and then removed (Wah). Du-Wah's were extremely popular in the music of Duke Ellington and later became common in many of the more popular swing-era big-band arrangements. The symbols for this technique appear in the music as a "+" for "Du" and an "o" for "Wah." The following exercise shows Du-Wahs as eighth notes and quarter notes. They almost always appear as repeated notes. In addition, this exercise begins with pickups, so the count-off will be different. On Track 40 there are four quarter notes plus the downbeat of the first measure. This is typically how it's done when three beats of pickups are needed.

TRACK 40

Exercise 14

At this point it would be a good idea to examine several big band scores to see if you can locate any of the specialized jazz effects we've just covered. Full scores by composers/arrangers Matt Dennis, Les Hooper, Thad Jones, Bob Mintzer, and Sammy Nestico are particularly good sources containing these effects.

9 Hearing Intervals in Minor

As with the major scale, all combinations of melodic and harmonic intervals are possible within the minor scale. The difference is that there are three minor scales commonly used for soloing, depending on which chords are being used. These scales are the jazz melodic minor, natural minor, and the harmonic minor.

The **jazz melodic minor scale** (JMM) corresponds to the ascending melodic minor scale in classical music. Another way to think of it is to lower the third degree of a major scale by one half step.

The **natural minor scale** (NM) corresponds to the natural minor and descending melodic minor scales in classical music. This is the same as the sixth mode of the major scale (the Aeolian mode) or a JMM scale with flatted sixth and seventh degrees.

The **harmonic minor scale** (HM) is the same as the harmonic minor scale in classical music. There are two ways to think of this scale: it's the JMM scale with a flatted sixth, or the NM scale with a major seventh.

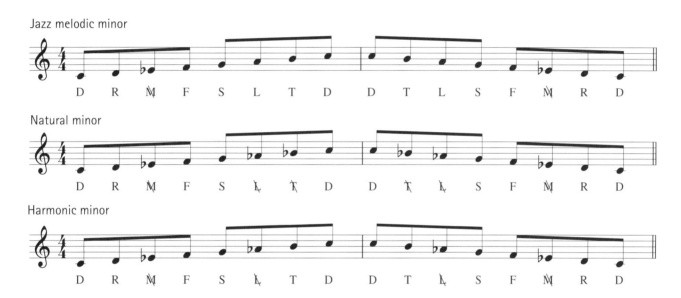

Learning Solfege Names for the Minor Scale

The following drills are intended to help you focus on recognizing and recalling scales, intervals, chords, patterns, and chord progressions found in minor scales without having to actually hear the notes played.

The Jazz Melodic Minor Scale

The jazz melodic minor scale duplicates the ascending form of the melodic minor scale used in classical music, but unlike the classical scale, the notes don't change when the scale descends.

The following block drill will help introduce you to the notes in the JMM scale.

Block Drill: The JMM Scale

1. Select any note in the middle of your vocal range and call it DO.
2. Sing a JMM scale up and down one octave (D R M F S L T D   D T L S F M R D).
3. Select a different note and call it DO.
4. Sing a JMM scale from that note up and down one octave (D R M F S L T D   D T L S F M R D).
5. Repeat steps 1 through 4 using a variety of different starting notes.

When you can do this quickly and accurately in eighth notes at a moderate tempo, starting on any note that is comfortably within your vocal range, you have completed the drill.

The example below shows what the drill would look like.

The Natural Minor Scale

> **Block Drill: The NM Scale**
>
> 1. Select any note in the middle of your vocal range and call it DO.
>
> 2. Sing a NM scale up and down one octave (DRMFSLTD DTLSFMRD).
>
> 3. Select a different note and call it DO.
>
> 4. Sing a NM scale from that note up and down one octave (DRMFSLTD DTLSFMRD).
>
> 5. Repeat steps 1 through 4 using a variety of different starting notes.
>
> When you can do this quickly and accurately in eighth notes at a moderate tempo, starting on any note that is comfortably within your vocal range, you have completed the drill.

This drill would look like the following:

The Harmonic Minor Scale

> **Block Drill: The HM Scale**
>
> 1. Select any note in the middle of your vocal range and call it DO.
>
> 2. Sing a HM scale up and down one octave (DRMFSLTD DTLSFMRD).
>
> 3. Select a different note and call it DO.
>
> 4. Sing a HM scale from that note up and down one octave (DRMFSLTD DTLSFMRD).
>
> 5. Repeat steps 1 through 4 using a variety of different starting notes.
>
> When you can do this quickly and accurately in eighth notes at a moderate tempo, starting on any note that is comfortably within your vocal range, you have completed the drill.

This drill would look like the following:

D R M F S L T D   D T L S F M R D   D R M F S L T D   D T L S F M R D

D R M F S L T D   D T L S F M R D   D R M F S L T D   D T L S F M R D

Minor Seconds and Major Sevenths

Minor seconds and major sevenths occur between RE–ME in all three minor scales, between TI–DO in the JMM and HM scales, and between SO–LE in the NM and HM scales. The HM scale is the only scale to contain all three.

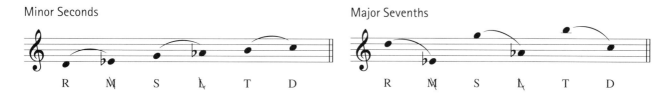

Minor Seconds   Major Sevenths

R   M   S   L   T   D   R   M   S   L   T   D

Block Drill: Minor Seconds and Major Sevenths in the Minor Scales

1. Give yourself a starting note (DO) and sing through the following patterns to get a feel for these intervals. Insert two beats of rest between each pattern. Start by focusing on minor seconds only.

   RMSLTD   TDSLRM   SLTDRM
   MRLSDT   DTLSMR   LSDTMR

2. Give yourself a new starting note (DO), start at a different place in the patterns, and sing through them again.

3. Repeat step 2 several times until the drill is easy to do.

When you can do this drill easily using minor seconds, begin adding major sevenths.

Interval Studies in Minor

The following interval studies are similar to those used for the major scale and should be practiced the same way.

Step 1

Write in the solfege names and practice the exercise until you can sing it accurately at a moderate tempo.

Step 2

Begin somewhere in the middle and sing through until you arrive back at your starting note. Do this several times.

Step 3

Imagine the exercise in a meter and sing it while placing accents on the downbeats of each imaginary measure.

When you feel comfortable with these interval exercises, move on to the next pair of intervals in the following section.

#1 in D minor

#2 in F minor

#3 in G minor

#4 in A minor

Major Seconds and Minor Sevenths

All minor scales share the first five notes in common. The differences between the scales are found in the last three notes, and there are many possibilities to choose from. The following shows the major seconds and minor sevenths that aren't already found in the major scale—they are only found in the NM scale.

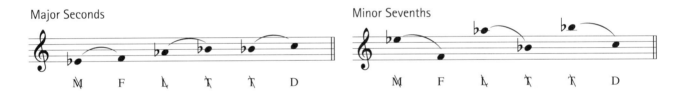

Major Seconds

Minor Sevenths

Major seconds are usually much easier to sing and hear than minor sevenths. Your goal is to sort out for yourself what makes each pair sound and feel different in each scale.

Block Drill: Major Seconds and Minor Sevenths in the Minor Scales

1. Give yourself a starting note (DO) and sing through the following patterns. Put two beats of rest between patterns. Start by focusing on major seconds.

   M̌F   ĽŤ   ŤD
   FM̌   ŤĽ   DŤ

2. Give yourself a new starting note (DO), start at a different place in the patterns, and sing through them again.

3. Repeat step 2 many times until the drill is easy to do.

When you can do this drill easily using major seconds, begin adding minor sevenths.

Interval Studies

Because there are only three new combinations, we have included FA–SO to provide more variety in your choices.

#5 in C minor

#6 in E minor

#7 in A minor

#8 in B minor

Dictation Exercises Using Major/Minor Seconds and Major/Minor Sevenths in C Minor

TRACK 41

Track 41 will play an interval pair with two beats rest before the two pitches are sung, giving you the answer in solfege. There are twelve interval pairs total. Your job in this exercise is to identify the interval and figure out which solfege syllables represent the pitches in the key of C minor. You may attempt this exercise in two ways: stop the CD track after you hear the piano-played interval and take time to figure out the pitches, then play the CD track where you left off and sing along with the voice, which begins two beats after the piano. The second way is to attempt the entire exercise in real time, without stopping the CD track. In doing this, you will have to identify the interval and solfege within two beats in order to sing it in unison with the singing on the CD.

Dictation Exercises Using Major/Minor Seconds and Major/Minor Sevenths in F Minor

TRACK 42

This exercise is the same as the previous, but in the key of F minor.

Minor Thirds and Major Sixths

Minor thirds and major sixths occur in different places in each of the three minor scales. RE–FA and TI–RE were taken up when you practiced this interval in major

The following are the interval pairs in the natural minor scale.

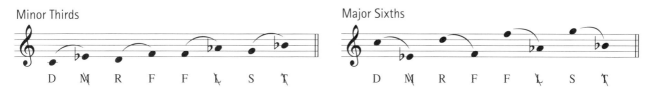

Here are the interval pairs in the harmonic minor scale.

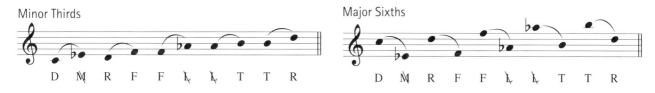

From the jazz melodic minor scale, LA–DO and DO–LA may also be included.

Interval Studies

#9 in F♯ minor

#10 in F minor

#11 in C minor

#12 in D minor

Major Thirds and Minor Sixths

These intervals are found between ME–SO, LE–DO, and TE–RE in the NM scale. They occur between ME–SO, TI–ME, SO–TI, and LE–DO in the HM scale, and between ME–SO, TI–ME, FA–LA, and SO–TI in the JMM scale. FA–LA and SO–TI (both familiar to us from the major scale) have been left out of these exercises so we can focus on the four new combinations.

Major Thirds

Minor Sixths

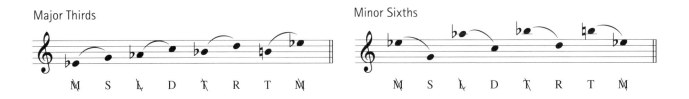

Interval Studies

#13 in B♭ minor

#14 in A minor

#15 in C minor

#16 in E minor

TRACK 43

Dictation Exercises Using Major/Minor Thirds and Major/Minor Sixths in C Minor

Track 43 will play an interval pair with two beats rest before the two pitches are sung, giving you the answer in solfege. There are sixteen interval pairs total. Practice this exercise as you did with Tracks 41 and 42.

Perfect Fourths and Perfect Fifths

These intervals occur between DO–FA, RE–SO, and SO–DO in all three minor scales. They are found between ME–LE, FA–TE, and TE–ME in the NM scale, and LA–RE in the JMM scale. Because there are many choices, in order to help us achieve our objective (to learn the solfege names for interval combinations in minor), we're going to omit DO–FA, LA–RE, and RE–SO, and focus on the rest.

Perfect Fourths

M L F T S D T M

Perfect Fifths

M L F T S D T M

Interval Studies

#17 in G minor

#18 in D minor

#19 in C minor

#20 in B♭ minor

The Tritone

Because there are three different minor scales, there are several tritone possibilities instead of only one. Tritones occur between FA–TI, RE–LE, and ME–LA.

In order not to get lost when working on the following block drill and interval exercises, we've add DO–SO to the mix. Because tritones are unstable, trying to learn them without a reference to DO is difficult.

Interval Studies

#21 in C minor

#22 in D minor

#23 in G minor

#24 in F# minor

Dictation Exercises Using Perfect Fourths, Perfect Fifths, and Tritones in Minor

TRACK 44

Track 44 will play an interval pair with two beats rest before the two pitches are sung, giving you the answer in solfege. There are sixteen interval pairs total. Practice this exercise as you did Track 43.

10 Hearing Melodies in Minor

The "Three Basic Steps to Hearing Short Musical Phrases" are the same for minor as they are for major. They are presented here in abbreviated form for review purposes.

Three Basic Steps to Hearing Short Melodic Phrases

Scan through a piece of music until you come across a phrase that you have trouble hearing easily. When that happens, apply the following steps to help solve any of the problems you might have hearing the music.

Step 1

Sing through the phrase as a rhythm exercise. In other words, chant the phrase. Pitches aren't important—rhythms and articulations *are*.

Step 2

Find a comfortable range and sing through the notes very slowly, out of tempo, using solfege. Treat the notes as a string of intervals.

Step 3

Combine the rhythm and jazz articulations with the correct pitches and sing the phrase.

Jazz Phrases

The following melodic phrases give you a chance to apply what we have covered so far in minor keys. These phrases should be practiced using both the swing feel on Track 45 and the straight feel on Track 46. On the CD, the first four phrases include the voice part. After that, only the drums are included, with bass drum parts specifically designed to go with the rhythmic character of each phrase. The phrases concentrate mainly on intervals and rhythms, but they also include many of the jazz articulations taken up in Chapter 8.

TRACK 45
Swing feel

TRACK 46
Straight feel

#1 in D minor

#2 in E minor

#3 in F minor

#4 in C minor

#5 in A minor

#6 in F minor

#7 in B minor

#8 in G minor

#9 in A minor

#10 in G minor

#11 in F minor

#12 in D minor

#13 in C minor

#14 in F minor

#15 in G minor

Several more exercises have been included that are similar to the first fifteen rhythmically, but have different melodies. You can use Tracks 45 and 46 to accompany your practice by turning down the voice track and using the drum kit accompaniment.

#16 in D minor

#17 in E minor

#18 in F minor

#19 in C minor

#20 in G minor

#21 in D minor

#22 in G minor

#23 in B minor

#24 in F minor

#25 in C minor

#26 in A minor

#27 in B minor

#28 in D minor

#29 in G minor

#30 in E minor

Hopefully this introduction to reading melodies in minor has been helpful. You should now have a better idea of how to perform some of the more common jazz articulations as well.

11 Hearing Root Movements in Minor

There are a considerable number of new chord choices in minor keys, all of which need some explanation. In addition to four different forms of I chord, there are two different forms of II chords, two different ♭III chord and minor iv chord, and at least eight different forms of V chord. There are ♭IV chords built from the minor sixth, half diminished chords built from the major sixth, two chords built from the minor seventh, and one built from the major seventh. What does all this mean?...Explanation to follow.

Minor Chords

The i minor chords with an added sixth or major seventh are easy to understand. They're very much like the I chords in a major key. The im7 or im9 chords have a minor seventh added. These chords are only referred to as i chords when they function as i chords, i.e., when they end a progression or are preceded by the V chord. When singing root movements, all these chords can be lumped together under one name; they are all "One Minor" chords.

The name for the iim7 chord is carried over from major—it's the same "Two Minor." The iv minor chord comes from the NM and HM scales. If the sixth is added, it's a "Four Minor" chord, and if the seventh and/or ninth is added, it is still a "Four Minor" chord. The v minor chord, called simply "Five Minor," comes from the NM scale. It's found in modal progressions, which will be taken up later in this chapter.

Major Chords

Major chords are found in unusual places in minor keys. The major seventh chord can be built from flat three or flat six in minor. The augmented major seventh chord, built from flat three, appears in HM and JMM scales.

Diminished and Half-diminished Seventh Chords

Earlier we talked about extensions to the vii diminished triad and stated there were two possibilities, but only one commonly used version, the fully diminished chord. That's true in minor keys as well, as long as we're only talking about vii chords.

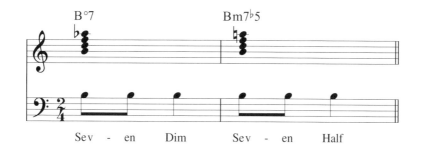

Sev - en Dim   Sev - en   Half

However, in minor keys the half-diminished chord is very common as either a ii chord or vi chord.

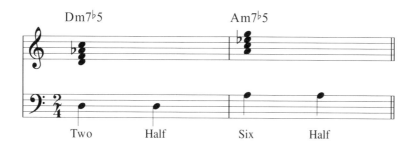

Two   Half   Six   Half

Remember, to sing a half-diminished chord, we sing "half" and drop "diminished" because it's the only chord in music that uses the word "half" in its name. As you can see, in minor keys this chord will be labeled as either "Two Half" or "Six Half."

V Chords in Minor

V chords in minor offer the biggest challenge. In addition to the fact that these chords can be minor in minor keys, there are several possible choices because there are three different forms of minor keys available.

The V chord in minor was discussed under minor chords, so it doesn't need to be taken up here. As for what to call the V chord with #4 or #II, use "Sharp Four" instead of "Sharp Eleven" because there are fewer syllables to deal with.

The last chord on the list is called "Five Nine Alt." The letters "Alt" are used whenever both the fifth and ninth are altered. It doesn't matter if the ninth has been raised or lowered as long as there is an augmented fifth present. This is a favorite chord for many jazz composers writing in minor keys. There's a special chord-scale which will also be taken up later to handle this chord: the JMM scale starting from TI.

The Non-Dominant ♭VII9 Chord

There's one more special chord that needs to be taken up at this point, the major chord with flatted seventh called the "♭VII9 chord." This chord looks and sounds like a V chord, but it doesn't *function* like a V chord. This is both because of where it's found in the NM scale and the fact that it normally moves up to the I chord by whole step. V chords and chromatic V chords resolve down by perfect fifth or down by half step.

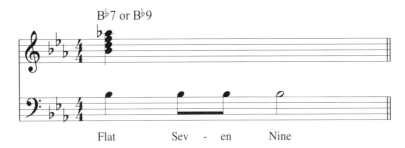

B♭7 or B♭9

Flat   Sev - en   Nine

When a major chord with flatted seventh functions as a ♭VII9, we call it "Flat Seven Nine," which tells us that this chord is not trying to be either a diatonic or chromatic V chord.

Singing Root Movements in Minor

The same three steps that worked for chord progressions in major also work here. They're listed below for review purposes.

Step 1

Sing through the letter names of the chords as a string of intervals. You can sing up or down from root to root, it doesn't matter which direction you go. The goal is to figure out how to move easily from root to root.

Step 2

Analyze the progression using Roman numerals and chord qualities. Definitely include the qualities in your analysis when working in minor because there are alternate choices. A ii half-diminished chord isn't a ii minor chord. Be clear about what quality of chord you want.

Step 3

Sing through the root progression naming the Roman numerals and chord qualities (write these out as needed).

Let's apply this to a progression in F minor. On Track 47, the voice sings the root movement line on the first time only.

TRACK 47

Exercise 1 in F minor

The only thing you need to do at this point is become comfortable with the new root names because everything works the same way it worked in major.

The following shows one more progression in minor. This one demonstrates the im7 chord as modal tonic, the ♭IIImaj7(♯5), the V9+, and a ♭VImaj7, all interesting tonal colors found in minor keys. Again, the process is identical with that for major chord progressions. On Track 48, the voice sings the root movement line on the first time only.

Exercise 2 in C minor

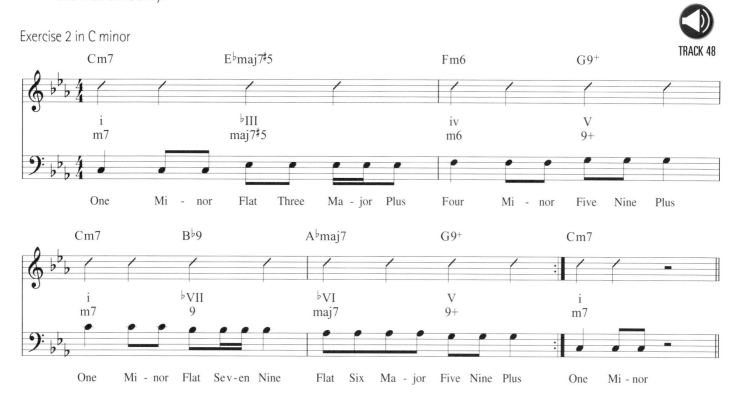

TRACK 48

At this point we have covered most of the essential material on how to label the various diatonic chords found in the minor scales. Now it's time to move on to hearing and outlining chords in minor.

12 Hearing and Outlining Chords in Minor

We follow the same procedure for outlining chords in minor keys that we use in major. Learning the names is our biggest problem because they aren't as familiar to us as the solfege names in major. The only way to overcome this is to start using them until they become more familiar. Obviously, the principal difference is that chords that were typically major in major keys aren't major anymore. And, because of the multiple choices that come from having three different minor scales, new chords appear that have no counterparts in major. This is just another way of reminding us that what we label something tells us a great deal about what it is and how it functions.

Minor Triads

In minor keys, the i chord is minor, but the IV and V chords may or may not be minor depending on the scale being used. For example, in the NM scale, all three chords are minor.

In the HM scale, the i and iv chords are minor, but the V chord is major.

And in the JMM scale, both the IV and V chords are major.

Because IV and V chords can appear in chord progressions either way, solfege names are what help us to identify these chords as major or minor.

DO–ME–SO equals a minor i chord

FA–LE–DO equals a minor iv chord

FA–LA–DO equals a major IV chord

SO–TE–RE equals a minor v chord

SO–TI–RE equals a major V chord

Major Triads

Since we took up major IV and V chords when we discussed major keys, we will only look at the new major chords that are unique to minor keys—the major chords built from the minor third (♭III), minor sixth (♭VI), and minor seventh (♭VII) of the NM scale.

Here's an exercise that uses these three chords.

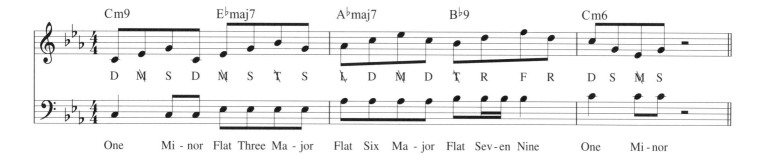

The Augmented ♭III Major Seventh Chord

The seventh chord built from the minor third of the key appears as an augmented major seventh chord in the HM and JMM scales because these scales both have the leading tone, TI, present.

What makes this chord doubly interesting is the fact that in addition to having an augmented fifth, it almost never appears without the major seventh being added. It's even more unusual because, in addition to being unstable, it adds a dissonant major seventh to the mix.

There is something special to notice about the root of the augmented chord built from ♭III. In this case we call it "ME," but when it's the fifth of the augmented V chord, the same note is called "RI." The sound of both chords will both be augmented, but each is quite different in function. The following example demonstrates how the augmented ♭III chord might function in G minor. Fill in the solfege names and then sing through the progression.

Diminished and Half-diminished Seventh Chords

Half-diminished seventh chords can be found as ii chords in the NM or HM scale and as vi chords in the JMM scale. In both cases, the seventh is a minor seventh (the triad is diminished, but the seventh is not).

The fully diminished vii chord, which comes from the HM scale, is different. The triad and the seventh are both diminished, making this chord act like a V chord—it wants to go to the i chord.

The following example uses a vii chord instead of a V chord to lead to the Cm. Fill in the solfege names and sing through the progression.

This next example uses both vii°7 and iim7(♭5). Fill in the solfege names and sing through the progression.

V Chords in Minor

Because there are three different minor scales, it's possible to find all the altered V chords of jazz as well as the unaltered V9 chord. As a result, there are numerous names and labels for these chords (most of which were discussed in the material on root movements in minor keys). The following example shows several possible V chords, beginning with the unaltered V9.

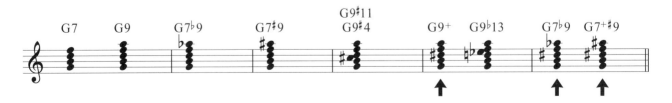

Even though nine different chords are shown, we only need two choices for outlining them. In these examples, if the fifth isn't altered, we use the normal SO-TI-RE (1-3-5) pattern. If the fifth is raised, use the SO-TI-RI (1-3-♯5) pattern. In other words, use the augmented pattern for the chords marked with arrows, because they all have raised fifths—the others don't.

The ♭VII9 Chord in Minor

The ♭VII9 chord in minor needs a little explanation. In the previous chapter it was pointed out that this is a very unique 9th chord because it doesn't function like a normal 9th chord.

As a result, this is the only situation where we don't want to outline a dominant chord by starting from SO. In this case we start from TE to show that, while it looks and sounds like a V chord, it doesn't function like one. So when you see the solfege names for this chord in the three-note and four-note exercises which follow, they will start from TE.

The next exercise is a summary of all the new three-note chords in minor plus altered V chords with raised fifth. Ascending chords are followed by descending chords. Sing through the exercise several times using different starting notes and shift octaves as needed.

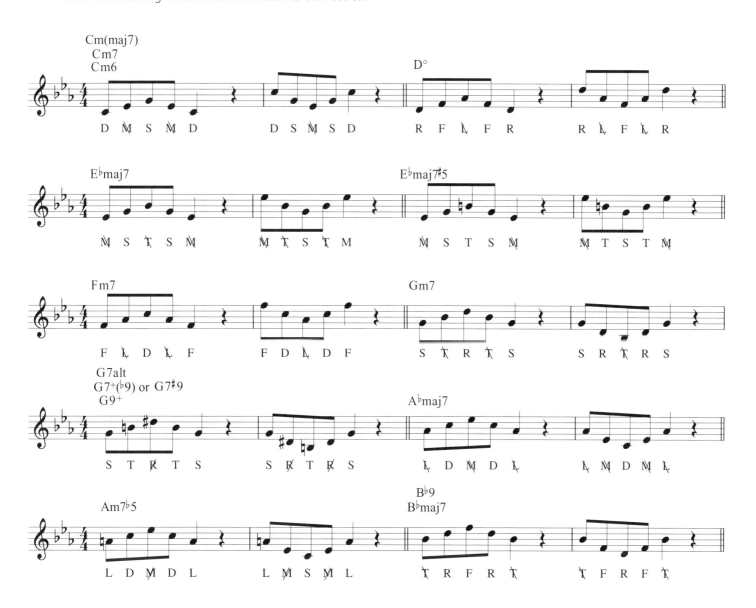

Modal Progressions and Modal Tonics

Sometimes chord progressions will use i chords that have a minor seventh added instead of a major seventh or major sixth.

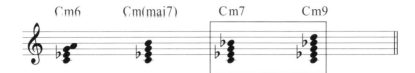

When this happens, the progressions are referred to as "modal progressions." Modal progressions became very popular in jazz tunes written after 1960, especially tunes in the fusion and jazz/rock styles. Both of these extensions are diatonic in the NM scale, so we treat them the same way we treat normal minor i chords. The following is an example of a short modal chord progression in which the i chord is a modal tonic and the v chord is also minor. Sing through the progression.

Since the Cm9 chord comes directly from the NM scale, it's a simple thing to make it into a modal tonic. But as long as we limit ourselves to only three-note chords, we really can't hear the difference that modal tonics create. For that we need four-note chords, which we'll take up next.

Hearing and Outlining Four-note Chords in Minor

The following exercise shows you how to outline the new four-note chords found in minor keys when chords last longer than two beats. Give yourself a starting note and sing through the exercise. When you're finished, give yourself a new starting note and go through the exercise again. As you master this exercise, begin to use these chords to expand your choices for outlining minor progressions.

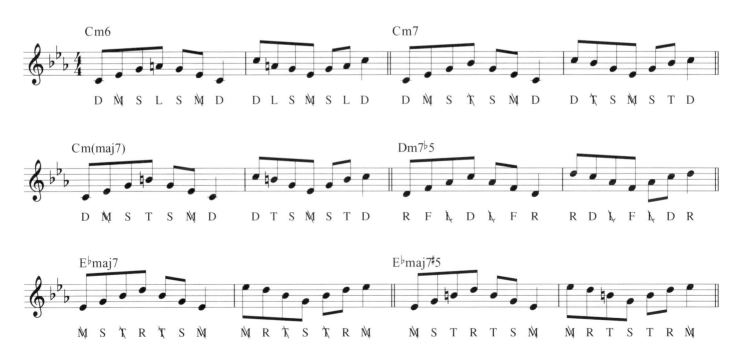

Next are some short exercises in minor that include chords lasting for more than two beats. Sing through the root movements first and then outline the chords.

By now, with what you have learned so far, you should be able to hear and outline almost any chord progression in minor or major.

13 Hearing and Outlining Inversions in Minor

The exercises in this chapter are designed to get you more comfortable using solfege while outlining and singing inversions in minor keys.

First Inversion Triads in Minor

Give yourself a starting note and sing through the following exercise. Repeat this exercise using different starting notes until you can do it easily.

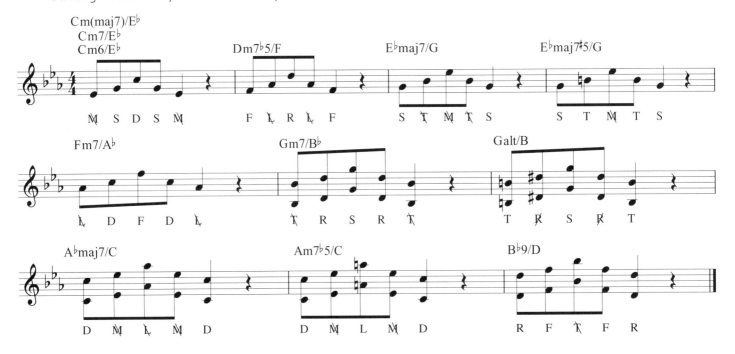

Second Inversion Triads in Minor

Give yourself a starting note and sing through the following exercise. Repeat any measures that you found difficult.

Remember that when chords last only two beats and call for inversions, your best bet will be to use three-note triads to outline them. As long as the extensions are diatonic to one of the three minor scales, you shouldn't have any difficulties, and if the chord is a V chord with an altered fifth, the augmented pattern will do nicely. Of course, when chords last more than two beats, four-note patterns become available.

Four-Note Inversions in Minor

First Inversion Chords

Give yourself a starting note and sing through the following exercise repeating any measures that you find difficult to sing.

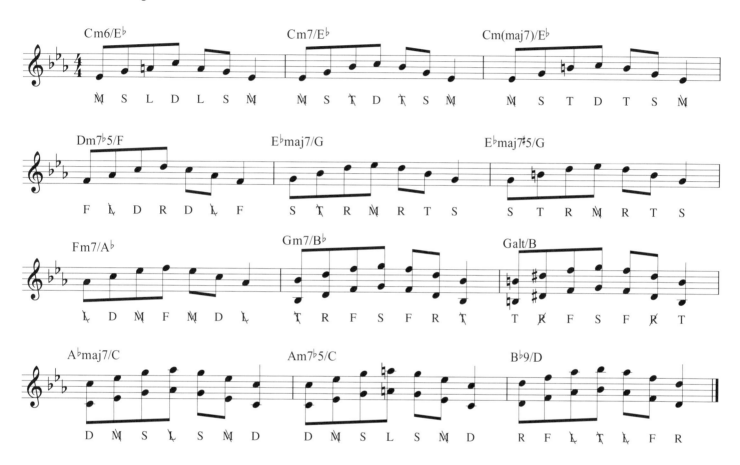

Second Inversion Chords

Give yourself a starting note and sing through the following exercise repeating any measures that you find difficult.

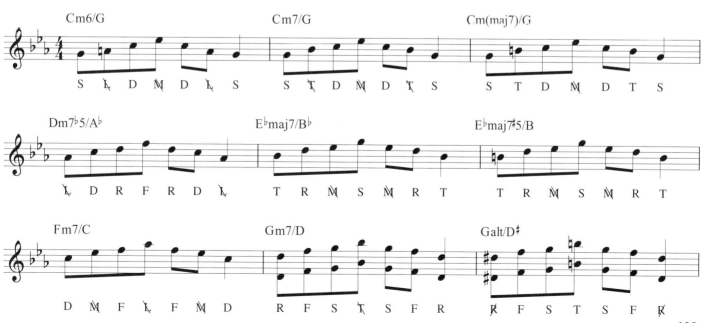

Third Inversion Chords

Give yourself a starting note and sing through the following exercise. Repeat as needed.

Here's an exercise in D minor that uses several four-beat patterns. Notice how the descending root movement in the first three measures is brought out by using inversions of the D minor i chord. This is typical of how inversions work.

Although this is a relatively short chapter, the exercises in it are very demanding. In general, they are much harder than anything you are likely to encounter in actual progressions because all the exercises, except the last one, use only inversions. But having had to deal with them in this way, you should be prepared to deal with whatever turns up.

14 Hearing Chord-scales, Part Two

Earlier in this book we looked at the chord-scales from the major scale. These were relatively easy to deal with because there is only one major scale. In minor there are three possible scales, and this makes things more difficult because there is often more than one minor scale choice for any chord.

Music theory has no names for many of the altered modal chord-scales that come from the various minor scales. Out of necessity, jazz musicians have come up with names for some, but the rest are left in a kind of musical "Never-Never Land"...they exist, but have no labels to identify them. The following charts illustrate the chord-scales found in the JMM and HM scales, with some of the names that have been associated with them. The NM scale has been left out of this comparison because all the modal forms of this scale already correspond to modes in the major scale.

Comparing the JMM and HM Ascending Chord-scales

Comparing the JMM and HM Descending Chord-scales

Dictation Exercise Using JMM Chord-scales

 to

TRACK 49   TRACK 61

The chord-scales are presented in ascending and descending form. The jazz chord-scale names are used for the answers (given at the bottom of the page). If you have difficulty recognizing a chord-scale, stop the recording and think about your answer before going on. If you make a mistake, stop the recording and sing through the chord-scale starting from the correct solfege name several times up and down to get more familiar with that particular chord-scale.

Dictation Exercise Using HM Chord-scales

 to

TRACK 62   TRACK 74

These exercises use the same format as the previous set, but because there is no agreement about names for chord-scales of the HM scale, the answers will only refer to the modes by number. Remember, if you have difficulty recognizing a chord-scale, stop the recording and think about your answer before going on. And if your answer is incorrect, stop the recording and drill the chord-scale before going on.

Locrian Minor

Before moving on we need to discuss one more diatonic chord-scale possibility in minor. This comes from the natural minor scale and is the only one you are likely to run into from that scale—it's the RE form of the NM scale.

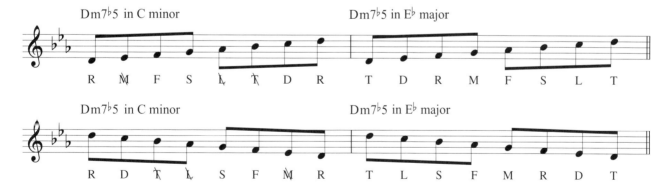

This chord-scale is the most recommended choice for the iim7(♭5) chord. It's actually the Locrian mode of the major scale, but because of how it's used, we prefer to start from RE of the minor scale instead of TI of the major scale, so the solfege names change accordingly. We call this the Locrian minor chord-scale to distinguish it from the normal Locrian mode in the major scale, where it functions in relation to a vii chord.

Hearing Chromatically Altered Scales

Altered Dominant Scales

Jazz musicians noticed that several of the chord-scales found in minor have very interesting properties that could help them deal with the altered chords they found in minor keys. Several of the chord-scales were useful in dealing with altered dominant chords (V chords). But two of the chord-scales they wanted to use—the Lydian dominant and the diminished/whole-tone—started from notes other than SO.

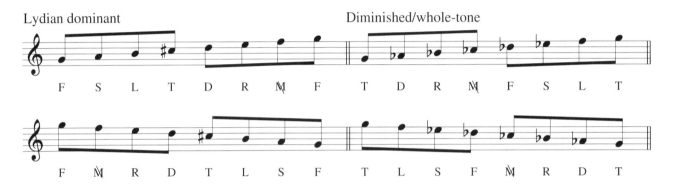

Since we treat all V chords as SO chords, regardless of where they come from, we need to change the solfege to reflect that usage. The following example shows the unaltered chord-scale from major, plus the four altered dominant chord-scales borrowed from JMM and HM, all starting from SO. The example shows their solfege names reflecting the alterations found in the chords they are related to.

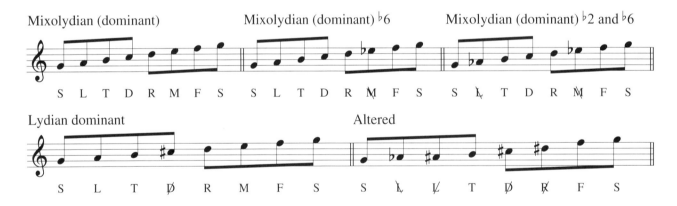

Here are the same chord-scales in descending form.

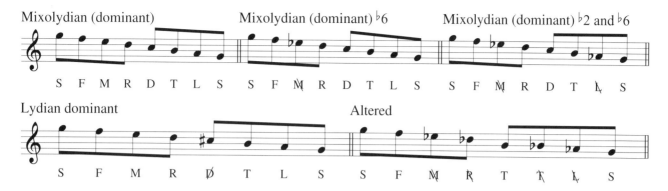

The first three altered dominant chord-scales use the same solfege names ascending and descending, but the final one doesn't. However, the principal notes that define the scale—SO, FA, and TI—are left untouched.

Here's a block drill to practice the descending altered dominant scales found in this group.

Block Drill: Comparing Descending Altered Dominant Scales

1. Select any note in the middle of your vocal range and call it SO.

2. Sing down the Mixolydian chord-scale, then the Mixolydian ♭6, Mixolydian ♭2 and ♭6, Lydian dominant, and altered chord-scales from the same note.

3. When you can do this quickly and easily, repeat step 2, but give yourself a new starting note for each chord-scale.

When you can start on any note and quickly and accurately sing any of these altered chord-scales at a moderate tempo, you have completed this drill.

The Eight-tone Dominant

In Chapter 7, we discussed the diminished scale, which is associated with the diminished chord. There is another form of this scale that has a different use. Several different names are used for this scale, including the whole-step diminished, the octatonic scale, and the eight-tone dominant (8-TD). We prefer eight-tone dominant because the name describes how many notes are present and the scale's function. This chord-scale is usually associated with a V7(♯9) chord. Normally, when that symbol is indicated, it's assumed that there is also a ♯11 present, but the fifth has not been altered. Here are some examples of the eight-tone dominant scale.

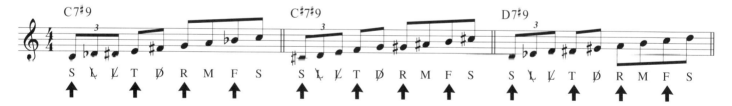

When practicing the 8-TD chord-scale, the first three notes (not the last three) should be made into a triplet in order to fit everything into four beats. This is done to ensure that the root, third, fifth, and seventh of the scale arrive on downbeats when the scale ascends.

When the 8-TD chord-scale descends, some of the solfege names change. DI becomes RA and LI becomes TE. Again, the chord-scale begins with a triplet, but this time only SO, RE, and TI arrive on downbeats. Nonetheless, most of the primary chord tones line up.

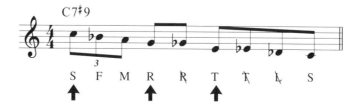

Here's a block drill to help you learn to hear the 8-TD scale and its resolution.

> **Block Drill: Resolving Eight-tone Dominant Scales to DO**
>
> 1. Give yourself a starting SO and sing up the 8-TD scale in eighth notes using a triplet for the first beat, and resolve the chord-scale to DO.
>
> 2. Using DO as your reference, change the name to SO and sing down the 8-TD scale, resolving the last note to DO.
>
> 3. Repeat step 1 using a new SO and follow it with step 2.
>
> Repeat the drill several times until you can easily hear and sing the ascending or descending eight-tone dominant scale.

Here's how that might look starting from G7(♯9).

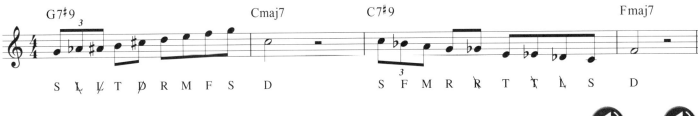

Dictation Exercise Using Altered Dominant Chord-scales

to

TRACK 75   TRACK 86

The chord-scales are identified as dominant, dominant ♭6, dominant ♭2 and 6, Lydian dominant, altered, and 8-tone dominant. Answers are at the bottom of the page.

Applying Chord-scales to Progressions

The most common chord formula in minor is the iim7(♭5) followed by an altered V chord ending with a minor i. The most "inside" chord-scale choices for these chords are the Locrian mode from RE, an altered dominant chord-scale, and a im6 or im(maj7) chord.

In the key of F minor they would look like either one of the following examples. Sing through all three examples to hear and compare different choices for this common minor-chord formula expressed as chord-scales.

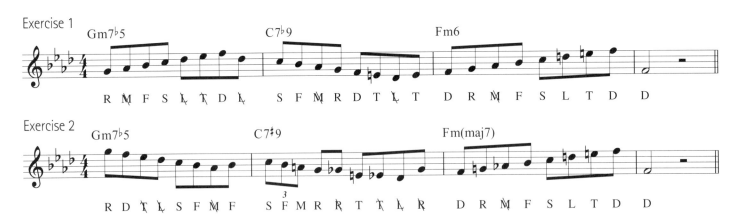

All you need to do now is apply this chord-scale material to challenging places in progressions as part of your practice routine. And don't be surprised when you find yourself using these newly discovered choices the next time you solo over a difficult chord progression, because the notes will already be familiar to you—you already know how they sound.

15 Hearing Guide-tone Lines

What is a guide-tone line (GTL)? Guide tone lines are melodies created from the thirds and sevenths of chords, arranged so they connect smoothly to each other. When we studied intervals in this book, we learned about how certain notes, like TI, tend to move up, and others, like FA, tend to move down. This is reinforced by the fact that TI is the third of a V chord and will move up to DO in the I chord. Likewise, FA, which is the seventh of a V chord, will move down to MI, the third of the I chord. Because of the predictable way these notes move, they provide a map of "guide tones" through the progression. In other words, if a soloist did nothing more than focus on the guide tones, every important chord change would be clearly defined. Of course, the solo would be rather boring, but there wouldn't be any "wrong notes" either. GTLs are, in a sense, a kind of musical map through the chord progression.

The first step in creating a GTL is to find all the chord thirds and sevenths in the progression and arrange them so that the notes connect to produce either stepwise motion or common notes. The line that begins with the third is called the 3–7 line, and the line that begins with the seventh is the 7–3 line. These lines tell us if the chord they come from is major or minor, and they also tell us what kind of seventh is in the chord. The 3-7 line is the preferred GTL to start with because not all chords contain a seventh. If you run into a chord symbol with an added sixth, use the sixth, or if you want, replace it with a major seventh. The point is this: you always need four-note chords for GTLs to work.

The GTL Bebop Blues

The following is an example of a typical bebop-era blues called "The GTL Bebop Blues." We'll use it to demonstrate how GTLs work. Of course, the first step we should always take is to sing through the melody to hear what it sounds like, and then move on to analyze the root movements of the chord progression.

If you analyzed the progression correctly and wrote in the root movements in the bass, it should look something like this.

Make sure your analysis is just the way you want it because later, when you sing through the GTLs, you'll be using the same words you used for the root movements. The notes for the GTLs will be different, but the analytical names, like the words to a song, will be identical.

Now let's create the 3–7 GTL for our blues progression. It's normal to start with the 3–7 line because most chords have a third in them, but not all chords have a seventh. So, in this case we start with the third of the F chord, A.

We move from A to A♭, the seventh of the B♭9 chord, then back to the third (A) of the F chords for measures 3–4. Even though the Fmaj7 becomes F9, the guide tone remains the same. Measures 5–6 return to A♭, the seventh of the B♭9 chord. In measures 7–8, the guide tones include the thirds of Fmaj7, Gm7, and Am7, and then the seventh of D7(♭9). B♭ starts as the third of the Gm7 chord in measure 9, then becomes the seventh of C9 in the following measure. The last two measures again move from third to seventh to third to seventh, finishing up the progression.

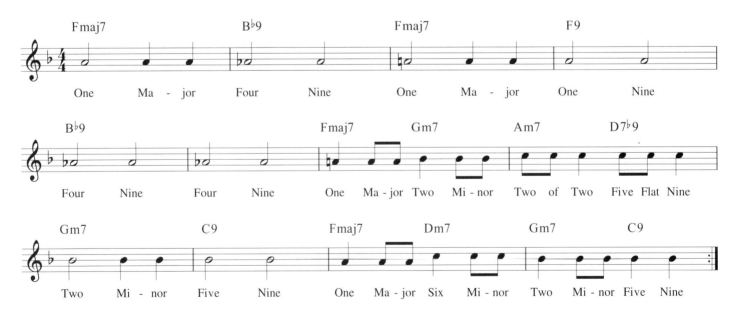

You can see that this GTL is made up almost entirely of half steps and whole steps. There's only one skip in this entire 3–7 line (in measure 11), one that should be fairly easy to hear.

The next example shows the 7–3 GTL for this progression.

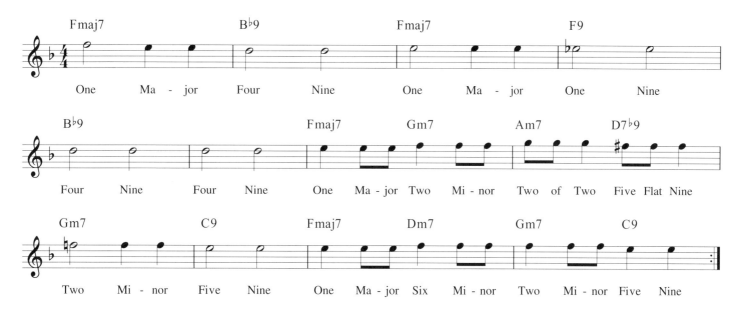

When a chord progression begins with a I chord and the chord symbol "maj7" is used, the best thing to do is start with the root and move to the seventh later in the measure. This is reflected in the first measure of the 7–3 example. For the rest of the progression, the 7–3 line acts much like the 3–7 line by repeating notes or moving stepwise, depending on what is needed. The one other time you might want to think of using the option to begin with the root is when the chord progression modulates (so you can hear the new root note in the new key), or when the final I chord appears at the end of the progression (and you want to end on the root instead of the seventh).

The next example shows what it would look like if we put the two GTLs together.

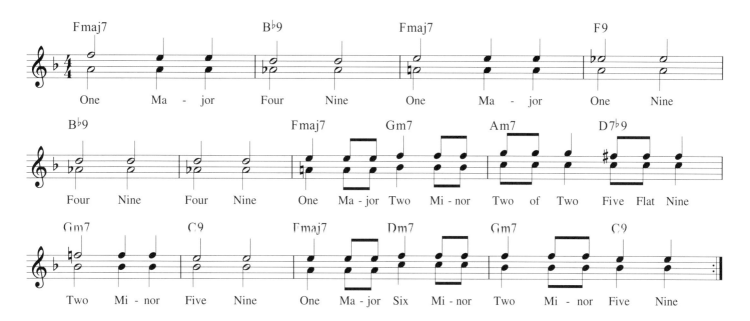

Next, we'll put all the components together, adding the root-movement line. On Track 87, the voice sings the root movement three times. Practice singing the root movement first, then pick one of the GTLs and sing it the second time through. The third time through, sing the other GTL. A I chord has been added at the end of the track to finish the progression. All you need to do is sing "One" at this point because we already know the piece is in major.

Since the words for the root movement and GTLs already define the functional analysis, we've left the Roman numerals out. You can include them if you wish, but they really aren't necessary when doing GTLs.

Good jazz soloists will often favor part of one GTL for one section of a progression, and then switch over to the other GTL for another section. Knowing both lines gives you that option. When you can hear either GTL easily while a progression is being played, you'll always know where you are, and more importantly, where you're going, because the next guide tone is just around the corner.

Season's Change

Next is a progression that isn't blues based. "Season's Change" is an example of a chord progression that is especially amenable to the creation of GTLs. As with "The GTL Bebop Blues," it is recommended that you begin by singing through the melody. To save time we've already written in the root-movement analysis for you. Notice how the piece begins with a ii–V–I formula in B♭. This tune moves back and forth between B♭ major and G minor, but always finishes on Gm7, which in this case is an example of a modal tonic. Thus "Season's Change" is in G minor, not B♭ major. Where and how a piece ends is more important with respect to its actual tonic than where it begins.

Season's Change

The GTLs for this progression demonstrate something quite interesting: no matter which line you begin with, the first ending leads you to the other GTL for the repeat. (Note that, since the root remains the same throughout both measures of the first ending, the GTL will use the same chord factor—either the third or the seventh—for the entire first ending.) For example, if you start with the 3–7 line, the last note in the first ending—B♮—moves directly to B♭ in measure 1, which initiates the 7–3 line. Alternatively, if you begin with the 7–3 GTL, you will arrive at F♮ in the first ending, which moves to E♭ to start the 3–7 GTL on the repeat. (Note here that we move F♮ up an octave from measure 7 to measure 8 to enable a smooth connection to E♭ in measure 1.) So, you see, in either case the first ending points to the alternate GTL on the repeat. Perhaps it is this melodic richness that accounts for the fact that this type of progression remains so popular with all levels of jazz soloists, from beginners to advanced veterans.

Now let's look at what happens in the second ending. Again we see a line showing that the two GTLs switch, only this time it's to keep the 7–3 line from going too low. GTLs normally descend, so when one starts to get too low to sing comfortably, we need to find a place where notes repeat, then leap an octave at that point.

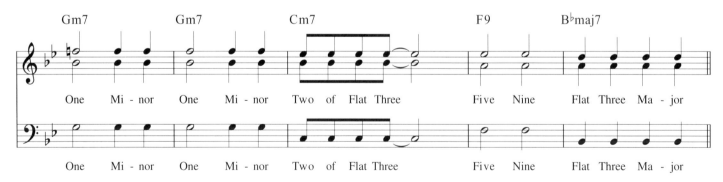

As we continue through the progression, we come to another point where switching GTLs becomes desirable. Notice what happens if we continue through the remainder of the piece without switching GTLs. By the time we reach the last measure, the 7–3 line (which is now the lower line) has descended all the way down to B♭ below the staff.

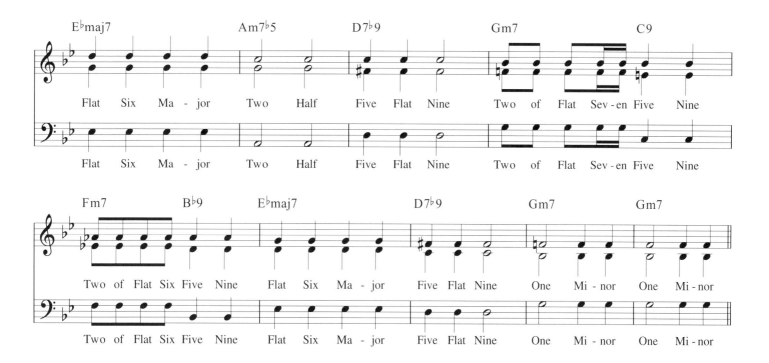

Now look at what happens when we switch GTLs eight measures from the end (measure 2 of the following example) on the Am7(♭5) chord. The range issues disappear. We do have to sing up an octave in this case, but it is worth it to help avoid the range problem.

This is a very sophisticated progression, but the solution—to shift from one GTL to the other as needed—handles the range problems beautifully. The following shows the completed 3–7 and 7–3 GTLs for "Season's Change," incorporating the line switches we've discussed.

On Track 88, the voice track sings the root movement throughout, one time through. There are several ways to practice "Season's Change." Begin by singing the root movement all the way through. Then pick one of the GTLs and sing it while the voice track sings the root movement. Go back a third time and sing the other GTL. At the end of the track, a i minor chord repeats in the last two measures. In the last measure, the voice track only sings "one" to signal that the last chord repeats. This is a practical way to treat tunes that end with repeated chords.

Season's Change

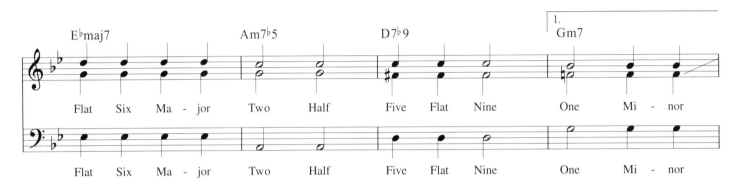

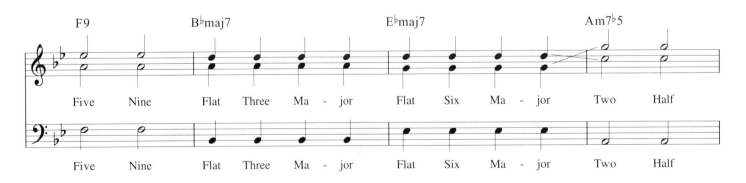

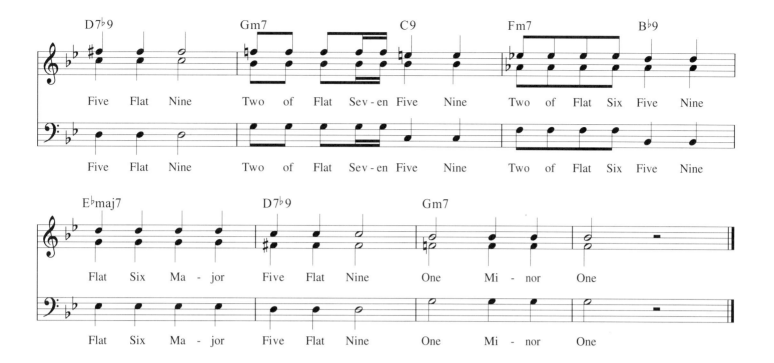

You will find more chord progressions to use for learning and practicing GTLs in the "Chord Chart Syllabus" section which follows. Some are adapted from well-known jazz tunes and others have been created especially for this book. All the examples should be worked out using the approach to GTLs presented here.

You can also begin applying this information to progressions in tunes you already know and would like to know better. Don't worry if you can't work out complete GTLs on your own right away. Some of the best jazz artists performing today—many of whom never studied GTLs formally, but have picked up these principles intuitively—will use GTLs for some of the more demanding sections of difficult tunes, and play the rest of the time drawing on their years of professional experience.

Thank You

If you've studied the material in this book and seriously worked at applying it, you've arrived at this page knowing a great deal more about ear training than when you began. We hope you have found this material both interesting and challenging. Ear training is a lifetime activity, and hopefully the tools presented here will help you considerably on your quest to become an outstanding musician—a jazz musician that others refer to as having great "Jazz Ears."

Thom David Mason

Chord Chart Syllabus

This section provides you with chord progressions to use in practicing the skills you've learned about in this book. Work on singing root movements, melodies, chord outlines, and GTLs. The first two charts are done for you. The rest have been left blank for you to work out on your own. You may fill in the missing elements on some, and/or try to sing parts such as the root-movement line at sight, without having the line written in ahead of time. Use the charts in a variety of ways to help you practice and develop your jazz ears.

The I–vi–ii–V Formula

The first chord chart in this section consists of a variation of the I–vi–ii–V formula found in songs like "I Got Rhythm" and hundreds of other well-known jazz tunes. The first example below demonstrates two of the most common formulas, often referred to as turnarounds. Both of these turnarounds resolve back to the I chord, so in this case they are "turnarounds to I." The top staff shows the chord outlines. Remember to use quarter notes to replace repeated eighth notes whenever you want to take a breath, or circle an eighth note and leave it out. The middle staff shows the GTLs and the functional analysis. The bottom staff shows the root movements. Note that the 7–3 GTL begins with the root.

♯i°7 and ii–V of ii

This second chord chart features two common substitute chords: the diminished chord in the first measure, and a secondary dominant in the third. Most musicians would analyze the diminished chord as ♯i°7, but others think of it as vii°7/ii. Both work out to be the same thing. In measure 3, if you think of the Am7 as iiim7 it starts with MI. If you think of it as part of a ii–V of II, it's "Two of Two," followed by "Five of Two." We prefer the second solution. Notice how the 7–3 GTL begins with the root, then moves to the seventh.

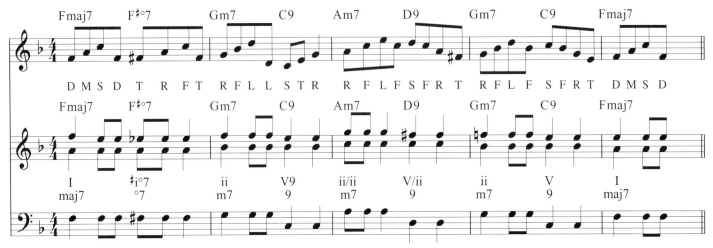

The Ladybird Turnaround

The next chord chart begins with a turnaround formula similar to the I–vi–ii–V formula presented earlier, but this time we have a I–V/ii–V instead. The third and fourth measures illustrate the famous "Lady Bird Turnaround" which gets its name from the fact that the first tune to popularize this turnaround was the tune by that name, written by Tadd Dameron.

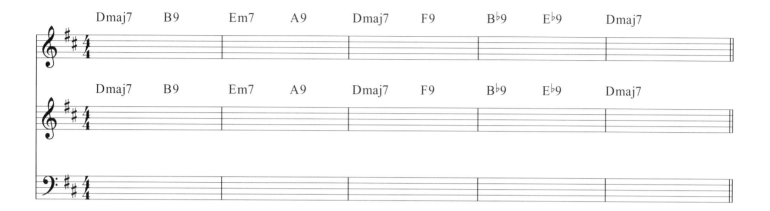

Descending Secondary Dominants

The next chord chart features descending chromatic secondary dominant chords. Only three chords are diatonic to the key: the I chord in measure 1, the V chord in measure 2, and the iii chord in measure 3.

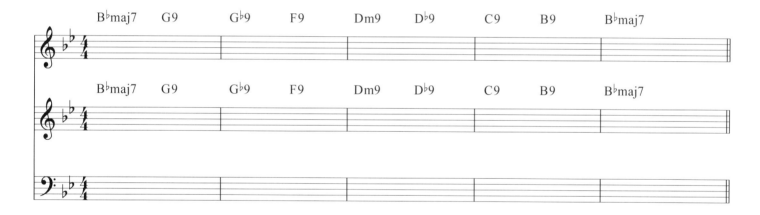

St. John's Island

"St. John's Island," similar to a tune by Sonny Rollins, is filled with secondary ii–Vs and variations of I–vi–ii–V.

Something for Alice

"Something for Alice" makes use of the circle of fifths in its progression. Each chord in measures 2–5 moves down a perfect fifth to the root of the next chord.

Indian Maiden

Charlie Parker loved to play a chord progression like the one in our next example at an extremely fast tempo. Practice it in 4/4 using quarter notes instead of eighth notes, then double the tempo and sing through the music in cut time. The first four measures have been done for you.

With a Mellophone

This chord chart, which is similar to a famous Duke Ellington tune, begins with a II9. It also makes use of an interesting secondary vii chord in the progression of measures 9–11 from IV to ♯iv° to Imaj7 with the fifth in the bass.

Is It Four?

"Is It Four?" is based on a chord progression used by Miles Davis. Most of the progression is made up of ii–V formulas that don't resolve to I chords until measures 14–15, where a complete ii–V–I in E♭ finally occurs.

The Moon Is High

"The Moon Is High" makes use of a progression similar to a popular up-tempo jazz tune from the 1940s.
Since the chords often last for a whole measure, you may focus on complete four-note chords for outlining.

Young Lady

The next chart is a jazz waltz in the style of the Bill Evans Trio. The sudden shift from the key of G major to E major in measure 9 is a dramatic moment in the progression. It stays in E for four measures, then modulates again.

Some Day

Mulgrew Miller wrote a stunning waltz on chord changes similar to those in the next example. What makes the progression so interesting is that you never really feel you're in E major even when you arrive at the tonic chord because the progression is constantly modulating.

Wait a Minute

John Coltrane wrote a very demanding tune similar to the next chart, based on ii–Vs moving in unusual ways.

Blue Samba

Though only sixteen measures long, this progression has become a classic. Treat the G7alt chords as augmented to ensure that the chord sounds altered to your ear.

Big Foot

"Big Foot" is remarkable because it only explores three keys, but they are all a major third apart. Singing three-note chords works best unless a chord lasts a full measure. Call the first chord "Sharp Five Major" because this progression is actually in E♭.

A Flower in the Forest

This is an example of a modal jazz composition with chords that move in unconventional ways. There's only one ii–V–I in the entire progression. Treat each m7 chord as a ii chord and you won't go wrong.

With Love, Señorita

"With Love, Señorita" demonstrates unique (and perhaps unusual) ways to modulate through several keys quickly. The progression begins with "One in Three Major," then moves to ♭III major in measure 4, ♭II major in measure 5, and finally to I in measure 8. Dizzy Gillespie wrote a similar progression that is usually played with an Afro-Cuban 12/8 feel.

I Loved You Once

"I Loved You Once" is performed as a moderately slow samba. Notice the rising chromatic bass line beginning in measure 3. Finally, since all the chords last at least four beats, you have the option to outline the harmonies as four-note chords or shift to quarter notes and outline the progression in cut time.

The Eternal Turnpike

This very demanding progression combines elements of famous jazz tunes by Sonny Rollins and J. J. Johnson, both of which are based on "Rhythm changes." Treat the first chord like a blues tonic and make it a I chord with a flatted seventh.